UNDERSTANDING
ROBERT BLY

Understanding Contemporary American Literature

Matthew J. Bruccoli, *Editor*

I, on my side, require of every writer,
first or last, a simple and sincere
account of his own life, and not merely
what he has heard of other men's lives;
some such account as he would send to
his kindred from a distant land. . . .

Thoreau, *Walden*

For
Carol and Billy

CONTENTS

EDITOR'S PREFACE

Understanding Contemporary American Literature has been planned as a series of guides or companions for students as well as good nonacademic readers. The editor and publisher perceive a need for these volumes because much of the influential contemporary literature makes special demands. Uninitiated readers encounter difficulty in approaching works that depart from the traditional forms and techniques of prose and poetry. Literature relies on conventions, but the conventions keep evolving; new writers form their own conventions—which in time may become familiar. Put simply, *UCAL* provides instruction in how to read certain contemporary writers—identifying and explicating their material, themes, use of language, point of view, structures, symbolism, and responses to experience.

The word *understanding* in the series title was deliberately chosen. Many willing readers lack an adequate understanding of how contemporary literature works; that is, what the author is attempting to express and the means by which it is conveyed. Although the criticism and analysis in the series have been aimed at a level of general accessibility, these introductory volumes are meant to be applied in conjunction with the works they cover. Thus they do not provide a substitute for the works and authors they introduce, but rather prepare the reader for more profitable literary experiences.

M. J. B.

PREFACE

This book has been brewing in my mind for more than a dozen years. That it has finally gotten written is the direct result of a series of debts which I should like to acknowledge: first, to Robert Bly himself, for writing the poems, essays, articles, reviews and translations which have interested, intrigued, troubled and challenged me over the years; next, to Ralph J. Mills, Jr., John Edward Hardy and Carl Rapp, friends and former colleagues at the University of Illinois (Chicago), who encouraged and supported my early interest in Bly; and to Ron Thomas, a current colleague, as well as the many critics of and commentators on Bly's work, both acknowledged and anonymous in the body of this study, and indeed, beyond it. Further, I want to acknowledge a summer sabbatical from Baylor University that allowed exclusive concentration on this project at a crucial time in its progress, as well as a Baylor University Research Committee grant that provided help in covering permissions costs. Also, I owe a special debt of thanks to Joe Flowers, who tames machines. Finally, and most importantly, I want to thank my wife and son who have provided the kind of continued, daily, and long-standing encouragement and support which understanding, as standing under, implies.

W. V. D.

ACKNOWLEDGMENTS

Grateful acknowledgment is made to the following:

Atheneum Publishers, Inc., for two lines of W. S. Merwin's poem "For Now" from *The Moving Target*, copyright © 1960, 1961, 1962, 1963 by W. S. Merwin. Reprinted by permission of Harold Ober Associates Incorporated in the British Empire and Commonwealth.

Robert Bly, for excerpts from *Silence in the Snowy Fields*, *The Morning Glory*, *The Teeth Mother Naked at Last*, *I Never Wanted Fame*, and a letter to the author.

Doubleday & Company, Inc., for excerpts from *The Man in the Black Coat Turns* by Robert Bly, copyright © 1981 by Robert Bly, and excerpts from *Loving a Woman in Two Worlds* by Robert Bly, copyright © 1985 by Robert Bly. Reprinted by permission of Doubleday, a division of Bantam, Doubleday, Dell Publishing Group, Inc.

East West Journal, for Robert Bly's "Mother Prayer." Reprinted with permission from *East West Journal*, P.O. Box 1200, Brookline, MA 02147. All rights reserved.

Harper & Row, Publishers, Inc., for poems and various other excerpts from *The Light Around the Body* by Robert Bly. Copyright © 1967 by Robert Bly. Reprinted by permission of Andre Deutsch Ltd. © 1968. Poems and various other excerpts from *Sleepers Joining Hands* by Robert Bly. Copyright © 1973 by Robert Bly. Poems and various other excerpts from *This Body is Made of Camphor and Gopherwood* by Robert Bly. Copyright © 1977 by Robert Bly. Poems and various other excerpts from *This Tree Will Be Here for a Thousand Years* by Robert Bly. Copyright © 1979 by Robert Bly. Poems and various other excerpts from *Selected Poems* by Robert Bly. Copy-

ACKNOWLEDGMENTS

right © 1986 by Robert Bly. Reprinted by permission of Harper & Row, Publishers, Inc.

Houghton Mifflin Co., for lines from "The Porcupine" in *Body Rags* by Galway Kinnell. Copyright © 1967 by Galway Kinnell. Reprinted by permission of Houghton Mifflin Co. Reprinted by permission of Andre Deutsch Ltd.

Alfred A. Knopf, Inc. for lines from Rainer Maria Rilke's "Eighth Elegy," of the Duino Elegies, from *The Selected Poetry of Rainer Maria Rilke*, translated by Stephen Mitchell, copyright © 1982. Lines from *Opus Posthumous* © 1957 by Wallace Stevens and from *The Collected Poems of Wallace Stevens* © 1954 by Wallace Stevens.

The New Republic, for one line of Robert Bly's "The Prodigal Son," published 31 January 1981: 28.

Weidenfeld & Nicolson, Ltd., for E. O. G. Turville-Petre's translation of lines from the *Hávamál* in *Myth and Religion of the North* © 1964.

Wesleyan University Press, for Robert Bly's "Where We Must Look for Help," copyright © 1953 by Robert Bly. Reprinted from *Silence in the Snowy Fields* by permission of Wesleyan University Press.

UNDERSTANDING
ROBERT BLY

CHAPTER ONE

Understanding Robert Bly

Career

Robert Bly was born December 23, 1926, in Madison, Minnesota. He attended a one-room schoolhouse in Lac Qui Parle County. After graduation from high school he enlisted in the Navy, where he became interested in poetry. When World War II ended, Bly attended St. Olaf's College in Northfield, Minnesota, for one year, then transferred to Harvard. At Harvard he became editor of the *Advocate*; met Richard Wilbur, John Ashbery, Frank O'Hara, and Donald Hall; read "the dominant books" of poetry at the time, Robert Lowell's *Lord Weary's Castle* (1946) and Wilbur's *The Beautiful Changes* (1947); and delivered the class poem at his magna cum laude graduation in 1950.

Having decided to make a career of poetry, and feeling "an instinct" to be alone after he finished college, Bly moved to a cabin in northern Minnesota and then, a few months later, to New York City, where he lived for several years, "longing for 'the depths'," as he said, sinking "as if through one geological layer after another."[1] During this time Bly read Jacob Boehme and Rudolph Steiner as well as Rainer Maria Rilke, Virgil, Pindar, and Horace. He began to write poems. In 1953 he moved to Cambridge, Massachusetts. In 1954 he went to Iowa City and enrolled in the M.A. program at the University of Iowa. His M.A. thesis was a collection of poems, "Steps Toward Poverty and Death." He married Carolyn McLean in 1955. In 1956–57, on a Fulbright Fellowship to translate Norwegian poetry, Bly discovered both his ancestral and his poetic forefathers: he visited his relatives, the Norwegian Bleies; and read Georg Trakl, Pablo Neruda, Juan Ramón Jiménez, and Gunnar Ekelöf in the Oslo library.

Back home in Minnesota, Bly continued to write poems and to translate. He founded a magazine, *The Fifties*, (later called *The Sixties* and *The Seventies*). In 1962 he published his first book of poems, *Silence in the Snowy Fields*, as well as *The Lion's Tail and Eyes: Poems Written Out of Laziness and Silence* with James Wright and William Duffy.

In 1964, as an Amy Lowell Traveling Fellow, Bly lived in England and Paris and met Neruda, Vincente Aleixandre and Tomas Tranströmer. He received a Guggenheim Fellowship in 1965 and another in 1972 and a Rockefeller Foundation Grant in 1967.

In the 1960s Bly began giving poetry readings and speaking out against the Vietnam War. With David Ray he organized American Writers Against the Vietnam War. He attended the draft card turn-in and demonstrated at the Pentagon in 1967. His Sixties Press had already published *A Poetry Reading Against the Vietnam War* and *Forty Poems Touching on Recent American History* (both 1966) when Bly donated the National Book Award prize money he received for *The Light Around the Body* (1967) to the draft resistance.

The 1970s were a productive and diverse period for Bly. He became increasingly interested in Freud, Jung, fairy tales, meditation, myth, the prose poem, astrology, Eastern philosophy, the dulcimer, masks (which he used in his readings in the 1970s), Great Mother culture, and the bouzouki (which he uses in his readings now). He organized annual conferences on feminine (Great Mother) consciousness, and, later, masculine (New Father) consciousness. During this period Bly published translations, two important anthologies, *Leaping Poetry: An Idea with Poems and Translations* (1975) and *News of the Universe* (1980), and several major books of poetry: *The Teeth Mother Naked at Last* (1970), *Sleepers Joining Hands* (1973), *The Morning Glory* (1975), *This Body Is Made of Camphor and Gopherwood* (1977), and *This Tree Will Be Here for a Thousand Years* (1979). In 1979 Bly and his wife Carolyn divorced and in 1980 he married Ruth Ray. By the end of this period, having mastered the first three of what he has described as the six "powers" of poetry (image, psychic weight, colloquial speech, narrative or character, sound, and rhythm) Bly said, "I felt I had gotten about half-way to the great poem."[2]

In recent years Bly has continued his almost frenetic activity, writing both poetry and prose essays, translating, traveling the country giving readings and lectures and holding seminars. His important recent books of poetry, *The Man in the Black Coat Turns* (1981) and *Loving a Woman in Two Worlds* (1985), further explore his continuing interest in male-female consciousness while his *Selected Poems* (1986), with brief essays introducing each section, provides a convenient survey of his career to date.

Overview

No poet of his generation has been more influential or more controversial than Robert Bly. No poet has ranged more widely in his interests or had a greater reciprocal relationship with writers and thinkers in other disciplines than has Bly. No other poet has written more important poetry in the lyrical, political, social, psychological, or philosophical modes or covered more critical ground in his essays and reviews. Because Bly's work has been so wide-ranging, his activity so exhaustive, and his presence so pervasive, he has become, in less than twenty-five years, the most conspicuous poet of his generation. To follow his career closely is to trace the major tendencies of much of the most significant poetry written during the past several decades.

Because Bly goes in so many different directions and because he is so prolific and, often, so unsystematic, even seemingly self-contradictory, he is difficult to categorize. No one, not even Bly himself in his extensive, self-analytic criticism, has succeeded in arriving at a convincingly systematic position with respect to his thinking in toto. The task is complicated, in part, because Bly has worked his poetry into the larger context of his other activities. Therefore, the individual books of poems tend to be yoked with the philosophic speculations of the same periods, and the philosophic apparatus both complements and in large measure defines the poetry contemporary with it. Thus, Bly is best understood in his various individual phases and each phase is best dealt with as a cluster of thematically and stylistically similar materials, separated from other clusters of a rather different sort which precede and follow them. Bly himself is sensitive to this approach to his poetry and to his work in general, and he often tends to group together like poems from different periods— many of his books are mini-anthologies. He also has the habit of returning to a few favorite thematic and stylistic modes again and again.

In 1980 Bly edited an anthology called *News of the Universe: Poems of Twofold Consciousness* in which he traced the progress of poetry from the eighteenth century, "the peak of human arrogance," to the present, poems of "twofold consciousness," and on into the suggestion of a "unity of consciousness that we haven't arrived at yet." In the poetry of the "Old Position" a "serious gap" exists between man and nature: "The body is exiled, the soul evaporated, the mind given executive power." The first significant attack on the Old Position was the Romanticism of Friedrich Hölderlin, Gérard de Nerval, Johann Wolfgang von Goethe, Novalis, and, in England, William Blake. "Insane for the light," like Goethe's butterfly, these writers wished "to die and so to grow" on the dark earth as the "troubled guests" they knew they were. Thus, by the beginning of the twentieth century, in a poet like Rilke, Bly finds "an area of psychic abundance" nourished by the German Romantics. This, he thinks, is the true source of major modern poetry and is quite separate from the Jules LaForgue, T. S. Eliot, W. H. Auden, Ezra Pound tradition. It is a tradition not of irony but of "swift association."[3]

Bly has always been able to find corroboration for his literary theories in other disciplines. In *News of the Universe* he adopts Robert Ornstein's speculations in *The Psychology of Consciousness* (1972) to the history of recent poetry. Since "the two halves of the body respond to and embody the modes of the opposite brain lobe," the left side, which "favors feeling, music, motion, touch . . . the qualities in us that enable us to unite with objects and creatures," have been trapped by the "bent over" body and crushed. The poetry of the last hundred years, then, "is an effort to unfold the left side of the body." But, since "war crushes the unfolding left side all over again," recent history has not been

UNDERSTANDING
Robert
BLY

by WILLIAM V. DAVIS

UNIVERSITY OF SOUTH CAROLINA PRESS

Copyright © University of South Carolina 1988

Published in Columbia, South Carolina, by the
University of South Carolina Press

Manufactured in the United States of America

LIBRARY OF CONGRESS
Library of Congress Cataloging-in-Publication Data

Davis, William Virgil, 1940–
    Understanding Robert Bly / by William V. Davis.
        p.   cm.
    Bibliography: p.
    Includes index.
    ISBN 0-87249-590-6.   ISBN 0-87249-591-4 (pbk.)
    1. Bly, Robert—Criticism and interpretation.   I. Title.
PS3552.L9Z64 1988   88-23662
811'.54—dc19
                                                                                    CIP

without throwbacks toward elements of the Old Position. Still, the poetry since 1945 has gradually increased the "unfolding of the left side" through several new "developments": the concept of the poet as shaman; the "transparent poem," similar to the poems of the ancient Chinese poets; the "massive movement of poetry toward recitation, toward words that float in the air"; finally, "the emergence of the prose poem," which is "the final stage of the unpretentious style" and of "the object poem, or thing poem," associated with the "seeing" poems of Rilke or the "object" poems of Francis Ponge.[4]

There are two reasons for detailing Bly's survey of the poetry of the last several centuries. First, it is useful to know these stages of poetic development as Bly understands them in order to appreciate and evaluate his critical and poetic perspectives. More importantly, this survey is important to an understanding of Bly's own poetry because he here rather clearly defines the stages of his own poetic development and ends his survey of the history of poetry at precisely the point where his own published poetry begins.

Bly began to publish at about the same time as the movement known as the New Left, which Paul Breslin rightly calls "*psycho*-political," appeared.[5] Both the psychological and the political sides of this dichotomy had direct and profound influences on Bly's early work and the psychological side, maintained with the fervor of its original impetus, has remained important throughout his career.

UNDERSTANDING ROBERT BLY

Donald Hall was one of the first to see how different from the other poetry of the time Bly's early poetry was. In 1962, the same year that Bly published *Silence in the Snowy Fields*, Hall edited the anthology *Contemporary American Poetry*. In his introduction Hall said:

One thing is happening in American poetry . . . which is genuinely new. In lines like Robert Bly's:

In small towns the houses are built right on the ground;
The lamplight falls on all fours in the grass.

. . . there is a kind of imagination new to American poetry. . . .
The movement which seems to me *new* is subjective but not autobiographical. It reveals through images not particular pain, but general subjective life. . . . To read a poem of this sort, you must not try to translate the images into abstractions. . . . You must try to be open to them, to let them take you over and speak in their own language of feeling.[6]

Hall is quite right in identifying Bly with a new kind of imagination and in suggesting that his poetry is not "autobiographical" but reveals "general subjective life." Indeed, Bly has always attempted to speak with a "profound subjectivity" and to make that subjectivity objective in his poems. As Bly says in an important early essay, "A poem is something that penetrates for an instant into the unconscious."[7] Later he added, "What is needed to write good poems about the outward world is inwardness."[8]

This obsession with inwardness has been present in Bly from the beginning, and it has taken various forms—some of them quite "outward." First there was the personalized private mysticism of his poetic beginnings in *Silence in the Snowy Fields*. Then there was the outward, public protest poems of his middle period, best seen in *The Light Around the Body*. Next, there was the attempt to plumb universal mythic consciousness in *Sleepers Joining Hands*. And, most recently, in *The Man in the Black Coat Turns* and *Loving a Woman in Two Worlds*, Bly searches out the "ancestors," both literal and psychological, which haunt his past, inhabit his memories, and continue to people his present world.

Bly's notions of "leaps" in poetry and of "leaping poetry" are important both as creative principles and as critical tools. He describes "a leap from the conscious to the unconscious and back again, a leap from the known part of the mind to the unknown part" as one of the necessities of leaping poems, which give off "constantly flashing light" as they shift from "light psyche to dark psyche."[9] Until recently such poems have come from Europe and the South Americans. American poets, Bly believes, need to relearn the poetic traditions which have come down from the "ancient times," the " 'time of inspiration,' " and from other cultures, even in our own time. This notion of the necessity for a "leap" in strong or authentic poetry is the basic tenet of Bly's poetic philosophy and the crucial test he applies to his own poems and to the poems of other poets.

Bly began his poetic career in the early 1950s when, in New York, he began to read seriously and in depth the poems of Virgil and Horace, Pindar and Rilke, the *Tao Te Ching*, Rudolf Steiner and, especially, the seventeenth-century German mystic, Jacob Boehme. Boehme, an obscure, difficult writer, borrowed his terminology from a wide variety of diverse sources and lived his life in a state of religious exaltation bordering on frenzy. His insight flashed back and forth between divine text and human contexts, and he saw himself as a vehicle for divine illumination in the common life of man on earth. In Boehme there are immediate parallels to the life and intellectual interests of Robert Bly. One need only think of Bly's essay, "Being a Lutheran Boy-God in Minnesota"[10] or remember his historical analyses of poetic tradition, his criticism of his own contemporaries, or his unique literary theories to find obvious associations between the dichotomies of inner and outer, body and spirit, conscious and unconscious, light and dark, life and death, male and female which are also in Boehme. Indeed, it is surely the case that Boehme, Bly's first major influence (quotations from Boehme serve as epigraphs to *Silence in the Snowy Fields* and to the four of five sections of *The Light Around the Body* which have epigraphs) has remained one of the most abiding influences on his work and thought.

It is this Boehmean influence, along with Bly's interest in surrealism and South American poets, which causes him to be associated with the tradition of the "deep image" or "inwardness." These influences, Bly himself acknowledges, make his "a poetry that goes deep into the human being, much deeper than the ego and at the same time is aware of many other beings."[11]

But Bly never seems to stop to take any stand for a very long time. Instead, he has constantly moved out into new territory to find new buttresses and new models for his philosophy and his poetry. In poets as diverse as Pablo Neruda, Cesar Vallejo, Federico Garcia Lorca, Juan Ramón Jiménez, Harry Martinson, Gunnar Ekelöf, Tomas Tranströmer, Kabir, Mirabai, Rolf Jacobsen, Rainer Maria Rilke, and Georg Trakl, Bly finds themes and voices which echo his own, or which he echoes. But it is in the work of the psychologist C. G. Jung that Bly finds perhaps his most useful and abiding sounding board. Jung had already defined and focused, from the psychological side, some of the issues and concerns Bly was interested in exploring in his poetry and thought and, as he had with Boehme, and as he would with other thinkers later, Bly was quick to make use of Jung's work for his own purposes. Indeed, Jung has been the most significant buttress for much of Bly's work in the last fifteen years, even though the clearest example of Jung's influence on Bly remains *Sleepers Joining Hands.*

The most overt use of Jungian sources can be seen in Bly's treatment of Jung's notion of the "shadow." For Jung, the shadow is the negative side of the psyche, containing "the contents of the personal unconscious."[12]

It is this "dark side of the human personality" that is "the door into the unconscious and . . . from which those two twilight figures, the shadow and the anima, step"[13] out into dreams and waking awareness. According to Bly "all literature can be thought of as creations by the 'dark side,' " and "literature describes efforts the shadow makes to rise."[14] These are notions which permeate Bly's work.

In recent years, Bly has circled back upon himself with an even greater intensity. He continues to give readings and make public appearances and continually finds ways to make his work and the work of others relevant both to the literary and the non-literary world through, for example, the organization of Great Mother and New Father conferences and seminars (which in some ways parallel the poems of *The Man in the Black Coat Turns* and *Loving a Woman in Two Worlds* respectively). He has also further deepened and refined the forms and themes of his poems. In addition to his continuing interest in Blake, Jung, Boehme, and Freud, Bly has, more recently, been attracted to the work of Joseph Campbell, the "three brain" theories of Paul MacLean and the work of the psychologist James Hillman. As Bly has said, "I learned to trust my obsessions."[15] Robert Bly is, if nothing else, a poet of obsessions, and any attempt to understand him and his work must account for these obsessions.

Bly's penchant for constantly revising his poems, and even his critical positions, suggests several things: first, he wants to remain open to a new, or more complete, vision of either poem or precept; second, and more importantly, he seems to be interested in documenting the final or more definitive versions of his visions, critical or poetic. Therefore Bly is exceedingly difficult to fix at any specific point in his career or with respect to any final vision, version, or revision because he is only seen fully in his final versions. In this respect, since he is still writing, and thus revising, one can never be certain that any critical comment will not need to be amended, or even contradicted, later on, just as Bly amends and even contradicts his earlier positions and poems. What this finally means is that Bly is interested in the developmental process itself and he recognizes that his work will not be finished until his life is. Although this philosophy and procedure may present problems for readers and critics along the way, it makes for reading and writing that seems constantly to be living and growing—the way readers are, the way Robert Bly is.

Notes

1. Robert Bly, *Selected Poems* (New York: Harper & Row, 1986) 12.

2. Deborah Baker, "Making a Farm: A Literary Biography," *Of Solitude and Silence: Writings on Robert Bly,* Richard Jones and Kate Daniels, eds. (Boston: Beacon Press, 1981) 73.

3. Robert Bly, *News of the Universe: Poems of Twofold Consciousness* (San Francisco: Sierra Club Books, 1980) 3, 5, 13, 32, 80, 81. Howard Nelson calls *News of the Universe* "a treatise on the history of human

consciousness in its relationship to nature since Descartes." (*Robert Bly: An Introduction to the Poetry* [New York: Columbia University Press, 1984] 75.) Richard P. Sugg calls it, "Bly's own textbook on himself." (*Robert Bly,* [Boston: Twayne, 1986] 121.)

4. Bly, *News* 124–126, 129–131, 210.

5. Paul Breslin, "How to Read the New Contemporary Poem," *The American Scholar* 47:3 (Summer, 1978): 365.

6. Donald Hall, ed. *Contemporary American Poetry* (Baltimore: Penguin Books, 1962) 24–25.

7. Robert Bly, "A Wrong Turning in American Poetry," *Choice: A Magazine of Poetry and Photography* 3 (1963): 47.

8. Robert Bly, "Leaping Up Into Political Poetry," *Forty Poems Touching on Recent American History,* Robert Bly ed. (Boston: Beacon Press, 1970) 10.

9. Robert Bly, *Leaping Poetry: An Idea with Poems and Translations* (Boston: Beacon Press, 1975) 1, 46.

10. Chester G. Anderson, ed. *Growing Up in Minnesota: Ten Writers Remember Their Childhood* (Minneapolis: University of Minnesota Press, 1976) 205–219.

11. Robert Bly, "The Dead World and the Live World," *The Sixties,* 8 (Spring, 1966): 6.

12. C. G. Jung, *Two Essays on Analytical Psychology* (*Collected Works,* vol. 7) trans. R. F. C. Hull (Princeton: Princeton University Press, 1966) 66.

13. C. G. Jung, *Four Archetypes* (*Collected Works,* vol. 9, part 1) trans. R. F. C. Hull (Princeton: Princeton University Press, 1970) 57.

14. Robert Bly, "Wallace Stevens and Dr. Jekyll," in *American Poets in 1976,* ed. William Heyen (Indianapolis: The Bobbs-Merrill Co., 1976) 4–5. See also Bly's recent book, *A Little Book on the Human Shadow,* William Booth, ed. (Memphis: Raccoon Books, 1986).

15. Robert Bly, "In Search of An American Muse," *New York Times Book Review,* 22 January 1984, 1.

CHAPTER TWO

Silence in the Snowy Fields and *This Tree Will Be Here for a Thousand Years*

S*ilence in the Snowy Fields* consists of forty-four short, often perplexingly simple, lyric poems. Bly's epigraph to the book, "We are all asleep in the outward man," is taken from Boehme and it suggests both the thematic thrust of the book and the structural arrangement Bly follows. The book is divided into three sections and moves from "eleven poems of solitude," through an "awakening," to an opening out, a movement "on the road." Thus, Boehme's "outward man" has been awakened from his solitude of self and begins the journey which will take him out into the world. The journey here is a paradigm for the journey which Bly's work in toto takes. And the voice of *Silence*, Bly's first voice, is his most authentic voice, the one he keeps coming back to. For these reasons, *Silence* is his most important book. It establishes the bases that allow the reader to read the rest of his work intelligently.

Although *Silence* is Bly's first book, he had a long apprenticeship. As he said, "I started writing in 1946 or

1947, so I had been writing for fifteen or sixteen years
before I published *Silence in the Snowy Fields* in 1962."[1]

The most obvious poem to begin a consideration of
Silence with is "Where We Must Look for Help,"[2] the
only unrevised poem from his M.A. thesis which Bly
saved for publication:

> The dove returns: it found no resting place;
> It was in flight all night above the shaken seas;
> Beneath ark eaves
> The dove shall magnify the tiger's bed;
> Give the dove peace.
> The split-tail swallows leave the sill at dawn;
> At dusk, blue swallows shall return.
> On the third day the crow shall fly;
> The crow, the crow, the spider-colored crow,
> The crow shall find new mud to walk upon.

Since *Silence* was a beginning for Bly and because it
has come to signal a new beginning in American poetry
as well, this early poem, based on the Babylonian Epic
of Gilgamesh, with its account of a new beginning in a
new world after a great flood, seems the inevitable place
to begin a consideration of Bly's work. But this poem
also holds an abiding place in Bly's most recent thinking
and, in this sense, serves as paradigm for his full career,
early and late.

In the Gilgamesh account of the flood three birds
are sent out to seek land. The third, the crow, following
the dove and the swallow, finds "new mud to walk
upon" (29). The reason that Bly chose the Gilgamesh

version of this story (rather than the later Biblical one) is because of this crow which, for Bly, symbolizes the dark side of the personality. As he said in a recent essay, "The poem came two or three years after college, and it seems to say that if any help was going to arrive . . . it would come from the dark side of my personality."[3] Although this dark side of the personality would not be fully explored for some time, this early use of the contrast between light and dark is important to *Silence*, which in many ways depicts a twilit world, a world of and in transition. And it is a complete world—the forty-four poems of the book should be read and understood as parts of one whole.

"Three Kinds of Pleasures" (11, *Selected* 35), the first poem in *Silence*, introduces "darkness drift[ing] down like snow," "white snow left now only in the wheel tracks of the combine," and "dark telephone poles" that "slowly leap on the gray sky— / and past them, the snowy fields." The darkness "drifts down" like "white snow," an interesting "combine," but one which much of *Silence* will be concerned with. The light-dark imagery, together with the sleep-waking dichotomy which runs throughout this book, suggests the conscious and the unconscious mind reciprocally interacting. It is important to realize that, for Bly, these dichotomies are not self-exclusive, and they do not contrast the positive and the negative. Darkness and sleep are as affirmative as light and waking reality, perhaps more so. Indeed, Bly often joins them in such a way that light becomes equivalent to waking consciousness, dark to sleep consciousness. In these terms light suggests the rational mind and an exterior, objective view of things, while dark suggests the subjective, dreaming, internal world. For Bly these two are incorporated or integrated with one another. In terms of his epigraph from Boehme, one must awaken to the inward man.

In this awakened condition, "we pass into a deep of the mind" (*Selected* 26). "At thirty-two," Bly said, "I felt for the first time . . . an unattached part of my soul join a tree standing in the center of a field. The tree's experience, existing without human companionship, and losing and gaining its leaves alone, was not unlike my own fragmentation, or estrangement, or unattachment. . . . In such moments, prepared for by solitude and reading, I wrote a kind of poem I had never written before" (*Selected* 26).

The poem referred to here is "Hunting Pheasants in a Cornfield" (14, *Selected* 29), where the opening line's question, "What is so strange about a tree alone in an open field?" is first answered by the body, which "strangely torn . . . cannot leave" the tree. Finally, "the sun moving on the chill skin" of the tree's branches focuses the poet's attention and draws into consciousness the parallel he first sensed in his bodily attraction for the tree. The last stanza reads:

> The mind has shed leaves alone for years.
> It stands apart with small creatures near its roots.
> I am happy in this ancient place,

SILENCE IN THE SNOWY FIELDS AND
THIS TREE WILL BE HERE FOR A THOUSAND YEARS

> A spot easily caught sight of above the corn,
> If I were a young animal ready to turn home at
>   dusk.

The mind, like a tree alone, apart even from the
"small creatures" around it, is happy in an "ancient
place," connected, growing from its roots into something that can be seen from far off, a kind of sentinel
which can direct one toward "home at dusk." The images implicit here are made explicit in "Solitude Late at
Night in the Woods" (45, *Selected* 31), where "the
body . . . like a November birch facing the full
moon . . . / reach[es] into the cold heavens" without
"ambition" or "sodden body"; and also in "Surprised
by Evening" (15, *Selected* 41) when "at last, the quiet
waters of the night will rise, / And our skin shall see far
off, as it does under water."

Dusk, twilight, is important to *Silence*. Bly has said
that "many of the poems in *Snowy Fields* . . . were written at dusk"[4] and many of them are set at that same
time of day. Surely twilight, dusk, is suggestive for a
man like Bly. Always interested in the shifting of things
and in the places where those shiftings occur, these in-
terstices become crucial to Bly's poems and to his
poetics.

One of the best known and most important poems
in *Silence* is "Driving Toward the Lac Qui Parle River"
(20, *Selected* 45). The poem begins at dusk, in a speci-
fied, particular place, and ends, not much further down

the road, in a moment of insight which typifies the kind
of "leaping" which *Silence* has at its center:

I

I am driving; it is dusk; Minnesota.
The stubble field catches the last growth of sun.
The soybeans are breathing on all sides.
Old men are sitting before their houses on carseats
In the small towns. I am happy,
The moon rising above the turkey sheds.

. . . .

III

Nearly to Milan, suddenly a small bridge,
And water kneeling in the moonlight.
In small towns the houses are built right on the ground;
The lamplight falls on all fours in the grass.
When I reach the river, the full moon covers it;
A few people are talking low in a boat.

One of several poems in the first two sections of *Silence*
which use the metaphor of "driving toward"
something—which suggests the metaphor of being "on
the road" in the third section of the book—this poem
makes out of a literal place, the Lac Qui Parle river near
where Bly grew up, a metaphor for his poetry. As Howard Nelson points out, the name of the river "has a
fortuitous appropriateness . . . the inward waters often
find a voice."[5]

SILENCE IN THE SNOWY FIELDS AND
THIS TREE WILL BE HERE FOR A THOUSAND YEARS

The first stanza of the poem is simple, largely descriptive, and seemingly straightforward. The third stanza begins that way, but suddenly shifts to "water kneeling in the moonlight" and "lamplight . . . fall[ing] on all fours in the grass," before it returns to the descriptive. How are we to account for these seemingly inappropriate and startling images in the midst of this otherwise rather traditionally descriptive poem? What is it Bly is trying to isolate here? How successful is he? The first thing to notice about the images is that they have to do with obeisance, deference, homage. The water "kneels" and the lamplight "falls on all fours," apparently to show obedience as well as acquiescence to powers beyond themselves.

These are the kinds of images Bly has become famous (or infamous) for [6] and they are frequently cited as examples of his poetry of the "deep image," a term coined by Robert Kelly and applied to Bly and others, even though Bly would probably prefer Donald Hall's notion of the "deep mind."

Perhaps the best brief analysis of the "deep image" and of Bly's relationship to it occurs in James E. B. Breslin's *From Modern to Contemporary: American Poetry, 1945–1965*. As Breslin points out, Bly's theories are not without their problems. The most basic problem is that once one commits to trust the psyche it is no longer appropriate to make judgments about the merits of individual images and, from a structural point of view, the craft of the poetic process is called into question by the process of the "inspiration." And Bly's theories are "oppositional and salvationist, at once impassioned and rigid." But, as Breslin says, "whatever their inadequacies as theory, they *were* generative."[7] "Deep image" poetry stresses feelings and emotion and, as Bly says, "trust[s] . . . the unconscious,"[8] but still does not exclude the intellect. The images, which often "leap" from one to another just as "the mind . . . thinks in flashes"[9] and which are full of "great spiritual energy,"[10] are often "irrational but psychologically 'right' " and express a "perception of inward reality"[11] that merges with the present outward reality of the poem.

Bly's "deep image" poetry is philosophically indebted to Boehme's notion of the two worlds. Bly's indebtedness and the essence of Boehme's notion can be most clearly seen in the epigrah from Boehme which Bly placed at the beginning of *The Light Around the Body*:

For according to the outward man, we are in this world, and according to the inward man, we are in the inward world. . . . Since then we are generated out of both worlds, we speak in two languages, and we must be understood also by two languages. (Bly's ellipsis)[12]

But Bly's most explicit, systematic statement on the image is in his essay, "Recognizing the Image as a Form of Intelligence," in which he says, "The image joins the light and dark worlds . . . when a poet creates a true image, he is gaining knowledge; he is bringing up into consciousness a connection that has been forgotten."

SILENCE IN THE SNOWY FIELDS AND
THIS TREE WILL BE HERE FOR A THOUSAND YEARS

Further, images "present intellectual evidence against
. . . the notion that human reason is alone in its intelligence, isolated, and unchangeably remote from the natural world."[13]

Thus, "Driving Toward the Lac Qui Parle River" can
be seen as a most successful "deep image" poem, or
perhaps even better, as what Lawrence Kramer has described as an example of "the contemporary poem of
immanence" which is "written to be a fragment of a
lost, privileged presence." In the first stanza, even
though "the time of the scene indicates transience, the
spatial relations point to a permanence of presence."
And, like so many of the poems in *Silence*,
"Driving . . ." vacillates between "observation and a
sort of descriptive rapture," often leaping "abruptly
from bare perception" to an almost "mystical vision."[14]

The second section of *Silence* begins with "Unrest"
(25),[15] a poem which introduces this transitional section
of the book and also looks forward to Bly's next two
major books. In opening the poem with the line, "A
strange unrest hovers over the nation," Bly anticipates
the political poems to come in *The Light Around the
Body*, and in closing the first stanza with the fragmentation and bifurcation of the "two shapes" which rise "inside us," he anticipates the psychological focus of
Sleepers Joining Hands.

Characteristically, the second poem of the section
gives the section its title, "Awakening." Here, the
speaker "approaching sleep," moves through "the long
past / Into the long present," through the "dark"

("dark" or "darkness" appear six times in the second stanza alone) to an almost apocalyptic vision at the end of the poem, where "the living" are suddenly "awakened at last like the dead."

"A Man Writes to a Part of Himself" (36) is found at the center of the book and is the central poem in the second section. In addition to being structurally central to *Silence*, it is thematically central as well and it points forward to Bly's most recent book, *Loving a Woman in Two Worlds*.

"A Man Writes . . ." is an early poem. Bly has recently discussed the period of his life during which this poem was written in terms of the poem:

I lived for several years in various parts of New York City, longing for "the depths," by which I meant the fruitful depths. . . . [I]n solitude I sank as if through one geological layer after another. . . . I lived in small dark rooms, and that loneliness made clear to me my interior starvation. . . . I managed to finish only five or six poems in three years. I saw the estrangement as a story: a man lives in a modern city, aware of a primitive woman bent over ground corn, somewhere miles away, and though he is married to her, he has no living connection with her.[16]

"A Man Writes . . ." begins with the evocation of a woman in a cave, grinding corn. This ancestral woman is "like a wife" to the man. He imagines her "hiding, rained on . . . starving, without care," although she raises her face "into the rain" to receive a kind of blessing. The speaker imagines himself "your husband / On the streets of a distant city, laughing, / With many appointments." In short, the modern man, busy with his city duties, finds himself "at night going also / To a bare room, a room of poverty." Like the woman in the cave he is alone and lonely, "in a room with no heat." Two questions end the poem:

> Which of us two then is the worse off?
> And how did this separation come about? (36)

The first question is obviously rhetorical since both the man and the woman are equally "worse off." The second question points to the need for the removal of this separation, and the integration of the separate sides of the psyche (here identified as male and female, modern and ancient or primitive), a task Bly has been increasingly concerned with.

Bly's use of the separation between the sexes to describe the separation of the psyche is basic to his philosophy and he has increasingly stressed it in his poetry and in his critical thinking, especially since his concentrated reading of Jung. Both men and women need to reconcile themselves to the other sides of their psyches before they can become fully whole. Thus the "part of himself" to which this man "writes" is the lost feminine side of the self which needs to be taken in and cared for "like a wife." As Philip Dacey has said, "A Man Writes . . ." "can be treated as a lens through which to view the business Bly is about in his work at large."[17]

According to Bly the "father" of *Silence* was the

twentieth-century Spanish poet, Antonio Machado. Bly translated a little poem by Machado:

> . . . our task is to die,
> to die making roads,
> roads over the sea.[18]

The third section of *Silence* is called "Silence on the Roads," and many of the voyages in this section of the book are over water, "roads over the sea." Such journeys become the dominant metaphors for the section.

The first poem in the third section, "After Working," begins, "After many strange thoughts / Thoughts of distant harbors, and new life" and ends, "We know the road . . . / The road goes on ahead, it is all clear" (51).

This metaphor of the road is basic to Bly's thinking and runs throughout his work, an obsession present here at the beginning and one he keeps returning to. "The Night Journey in the Cooking Pot," from *Sleepers Joining Hands*, begins "I was born during the night sea-journey" and "I felt the road first in New York,"[19] referring to his early period of solitude and isolation. In "The Fire of Despair Has Been Our Saviour," from *The Light Around the Body*, Bly asks, "Where has the road gone?"[20] And although these poems appear after *Silence*, at least one of them, "The Fire of Despair . . ." was written much earlier (many of the poems of *Light* were written earlier than the poems of *Silence*). Bly has said, "The poem in *Light* which asks, 'Where has the road gone?' was written about ten years before the poem that says, 'We know the road.' "[21] And, again typical of Bly, he has recently further revised "The Fire of Despair . . ." in his *Selected Poems* (14) and placed this new version of the poem in the early section of the book, along with the other poems he associates with the New York period. This section of *Selected Poems* Bly calls, appropriately enough, "The Road of Poverty and Death"—an interesting revision in terms of the metaphor of the road and of the title of his M.A. thesis, "Steps Toward Poverty and Death."

This obsession with a single metaphor through various versions of a single poem spanning more than thirty years is typical of Bly. There is no reason to believe that he has finished revising this poem, or any other. In this sense, what is most important for Bly is always the most recent version of the vision of an idea or a poem, and he has no qualms about changing earlier versions of poems or essays to coincide with his most recent thinking. Everything always seems tentative. Ultimately Bly is more interested in the development, the process of his thought, than with fixing it firmly at any individual point along the way. This tendency and practice must constantly be kept in mind when reading him.

"Old Boards" (57) is a particularly interesting and important poem. The opening lines:

> I love to see boards lying on the ground in early spring:
> The ground beneath them is wet and muddy—

evoke images of new life similar to the images in "Where We Must Look For Help" and also suggest the

metaphor of the road dominant in this section of *Silence*.
The "road" here is over water. The boards, lying over
the wet ground, provide a road over water just as the
ark in the earlier poem traveled a "road" over water:
"This is wood one sees on the decks of ocean ships, /
Wood that carries us far from land." The boards themselves come to symbolize the road, the journey of the
man who walks upon them:

> This wood is like a man who has a simple life,
> Living through the spring and winter on the ship
>   of his own desire.

This section of *Silence* is typical of the way Bly builds up
an idea in a series of poems, utilizing several basic images that expand, sometimes in surprising or seemingly
irrelevant ways (i.e., the "sleek black water beetle" at
the end of "Night" [55], which is another kind of "journey" over water).

What can be seen at work here in Bly is important to
an understanding of his poems, and to an understanding of other poets writing at about this same period. As
Charles Molesworth has explained, "the dominant
sense of a poem as an autotelic, self-explaining statement, or 'object,' began to lose its force" in the 1950s
and "in its place in the late fifties and early sixties"
three "other images of the poem" came into promi-
nence: "1) the poem as force-field; 2) the poem as a
'leaping' or associatively linked cluster of nondiscursive
images; and 3) the poem as commentary on some un-
spoken myth."[22]

SILENCE IN THE SNOWY FIELDS AND
THIS TREE WILL BE HERE FOR A THOUSAND YEARS

If it is the case that "Something [or someone] homeless is looking on the long roads" ("Silence" in *Silence* [59], revised and retitled "Uneasiness in Fall" in *Selected* [30]) for home here, this journey comes to a powerful conclusion with "Snowfall in the Afternoon" (60), the final poem of the book, a poem Bly associated with "Where We Must Look for Help" (under the heading "Problems of the Ark") in *A Little Book on the Human Shadow*.[23] Here again there are the pervasive symbols of *Silence*: the "darkness," a darkness "always there, which we never noticed"; the snow which "starts in late afternoon" at or near dusk and "grows heavier"; but added to these symbols so typical of *Silence* there is the strange image of the barn "moving toward us":

Like a hulk blown toward us in a storm at sea;
All the sailors on deck have been blind for many
    years.

The poem begins in the present ("The grass is half-covered with snow") but, immediately, the past is evoked ("It was the sort of snowfall that starts in late afternoon") and, then again, in the third line of the opening tercet, the poem returns to the present ("And now the little houses of the grass are growing dark"). From this point onward, from the taking up of "handfuls of darkness" in the second tercet to the blind sailors in the fourth, the poem explores the vision, the darkness, the snow, and the journey that the whole of *Silence* has been exploring.

But there is still the haunting images of the last three lines of this poem and this book. Things are "moving toward us" here at the end of "Snowfall" and *Silence*. First there is the barn "full of corn." Corn has appeared throughout the book, most surrealistically in "Approaching Winter" (19) where "The corn is wandering in dark corridors, / Near the well and the whisper of tombs" and "the corn leaves scrape their feet on the wind." Then there is the barn itself, a land-bound structure (imagined to be moving because the snow seems to decrease the distance between things) that is transformed into a water-going "hulk" being blown fitfully "toward us in a storm," unable to be controlled by its sailors who have been "blind for many years." Surely, this is an ominous image, although it seems not a threatening one. The blind sailors seem to steer their ship not by outward vision, but by an inner vision or insight, and although the book ends with this image of a storm on a winter sea, there seems to be the inevitability of a calm to follow—or, if the "storm at sea" is interpreted in terms of the visionary metaphor of the poem, as a pun on vision itself, then both the poem and the book end with the speaker staring out to sea, to see.

* * *

Although Bly has written " 'snowy fields' poems without pause, maybe eight or nine a year"[24] he didn't publish another collection of them until 1975 when twenty "snowy fields" poems appeared in *Old Man Rubbing His Eyes*.[25] In 1979 Bly added an additional

twenty-four poems to the *Old Man* collection and published *This Tree Will Be Here for a Thousand Years*.[26] In an
introductory note he said, "These poems . . . form a
volume added to *Silence in the Snowy Fields*; the two
books make one book. . . ."[27] In his *Selected Poems* Bly
promises that "a third group [of "snowy fields poems"]
will be published later."[28]

This Tree is like *Silence*, then, in thematic ways, and
it is like it in structural ways as well. Both books contain
forty-four short lyric poems and both represent a journey. The journey in *Silence* is outward, and chronological, from solitude to "the road," while the journey in
This Tree is circular and cyclical, a journey through the
cycle of a year beginning in fall and ending in winter.
But what is ultimately important is that *This Tree* represents a distinct stage in the development of Bly's career.
The poems here, beyond their associations with the poems of *Silence*, are deeper and darker poems. There is in
them "an energy circling downward" (10) which suggests a crucial turn toward the father and a growing
sense of man's mortality just as, in his earlier work, Bly
had been more drawn toward mother figures and im-
mortal nature.

The theme of mortality is pervasive in *This Tree*. It is
described not only in terms of death, but in terms of
absence. Indeed, even more than things disappearing,
things "disappeared" make for a constant presence of
absence in the book. In this respect Bly, like many of his
contemporaries, would agree with W. S. Merwin: "Tell
me what you see vanishing and I / Will tell you who

you are."[29] As one critic has said, *This Tree* is "constantly envisioning things at a vanishing point."[30]

A sense of loss is immediately evident in *This Tree*. In the first poem in the book, "October Frost," "Our ears hear tinier sounds / reaching far away east in the early darkness" (17) and in "To Live" we read, "To live is to rush ahead eating up your own death"(25). In short, the sense of things vanishing in *This Tree* represents a contrast to and a source of comparison with *Silence*. The poems in *This Tree* tend to describe the process, already completed, which the poems of *Silence* begin.

This Tree has occasioned some of the most contradictory criticism Bly has received. For instance, in "Women We Never See Again," (41) several critics have cited the same sentence for quite different reasons. Bly's lines, "Sometimes when you put your hand into a hollow tree / you touch the dark places between the stars"(41) has been called "a remark that might be charming if uttered by a 6-year-old,"[31] while another critic says about the lines, "Not many of Bly's readers have done that, I imagine, but I . . . *have* done it. I'm damned if he isn't right."[32] Yet another critic suggests that "such intuitive moments . . . are perhaps the principal reward of *Tree*."[33] Finally, Kramer, having called the hollow in the tree "a site of sudden epiphany," cites the lines as conclusion to his argument of the thesis of much of Bly's work:

Bly's aim in *Tree* is to find a severe simplicity by submitting attention to a drastic discipline. He looks

SILENCE IN THE SNOWY FIELDS AND
THIS TREE WILL BE HERE FOR A THOUSAND YEARS

into his privileged landscape to single out two or three objects, not necessarily related ones, which animate each other . . . merely by existing together. The objects all belong to the life of rural work and its seasonal imperatives; they are all somehow innocent; and they are all sanctified by their participation in the primary mystery of natural space: "Sometimes when you put your hand . . ."[34]

This Tree is Bly's attempt to return to his beginnings, in both a personal and a poetic way. In this sense it is a book of renewal, the return and beginning again most writers go through in mid-career. But, for all the thematic and structural similarities, *This Tree* is different from *Silence*. It is a darker beginning, filled with shadows and sorrow, the book of a man who has turned toward home and toward death. In the second poem in the book entitled "Writing Again," Bly, after saying how he has spent his day, asks himself, "And what good will it do me in the grave?"(18). Having spent his days, for years, writing poems, what good has he done, for himself or others? This is the question which lies behind many of the poems in *This Tree*. What lasts? The right kind of tree may last a thousand years. But even the pine in the epigraph from Tao Yuan-Ming, which "has found a place to be" and for a thousand years "will not give up this place," "still throws a full shadow," and is mortal and dying, just as the poet is. Even though he compares himself to the tree, "I too am a dark shape vertical to the earth" (54), he knows what is ahead of him.

"Reading in Fall Rain" (23) makes explicit the contrast between *This Tree* and *Silence*. It begins, "The fields are black once more," (i.e. the harvest is in), the "snowy fields" are still to come. And the speaker "reach[es] out with open arms / To pull in the black fields." He "feel[s] like a butterfly / joyful in its powerful cocoon," although still unborn. And then, as in so many of these poems, there is a sudden epiphany, a revelation or flash of insight, "one of my bodies is gone!" Whatever this is, "walking / swiftly away in the rain," is the second "presence" or "second consciousness" Bly has spoken of in the introduction to the book, a "consciousness *out there.*" (9) He said, "Each of the poems that follow contains an instant, sometimes twenty seconds long, sometimes longer, when I was aware of two separate energies: my own consciousness . . . and a second consciousness. . . . I've come to believe . . . that it is important for everyone that the second consciousness appear somehow in the poem"(9–10).

Because this book is so much a return to beginnings and a looking forward toward ends, the poem "Driving My Parents Home at Christmas" (47), which puts these questions specifically in terms of the immediate life of Robert Bly, is particularly important.

As I drive my parents home through the snow,
their frailty hesitates on the edge of a mountainside.
I call over the cliff,
only snow answers.
They talk quietly
of hauling water, of eating an orange,

SILENCE IN THE SNOWY FIELDS AND
THIS TREE WILL BE HERE FOR A THOUSAND YEARS

of a grandchild's photograph left behind last night.
When they open the door of their house, they disappear.
And the oak when it falls in the forest who hears it
   through the miles and miles of silence?
They sit so close to each other . . . as if pressed together
   by the snow (Bly's ellipsis).

Here, at the time of the holiday which celebrates
new life and the promise of the future, the poet takes
his frail parents home through snow. His parents, content in the cocoon (a pervasive symbol in the book) of
the car (a vehicle often referred to in these poems),
speak quietly of small matters, which matter a great
deal to them in the reduced realm of their world. Then,
"When they open the door of their house, they disappear." This is more than literal statement; Bly and his
parents are at the stage in life where every exit, every
leave-taking is symbolic of the final leave-taking, a
present absence like the sound of a tree falling in a forest when no one is there to hear it. The parents enter
the house and disappear, but they are remembered by
their son as sitting so closely together that they seem to
be already at home in the universe, "as if pressed together by the snow." The poem begins by focusing on
the speaker, the son, the "I" ("As I drive . . . ," "I
call . . ."); but it ends by focusing on the parents,
"they" ("They talk . . . ," "They sit . . . ," "they disappear"). The symbolic and imminent disappearance of
the parents, the poet's literal origin, simultaneously
suggests the emptiness ahead of him and behind him.

"Late Moon," likewise, places the poet before the door of his father's house, and "As I turn to go in, I see my shadow reach for the latch"(57). The constant pressure of the void is persistent throughout *This Tree*. It is most definitively seen in "The Empty Place" (51, revised in *Selected*, 48). The revised version will be used for this discussion.

"The Empty Place" begins with a prose statement that celebrates "empty places." They are "white and light-footed"; there is "a joy in emptiness." Empty places are "a place to live." This prose statement, set off from the poem proper and put in italics, reads like a sacred text that the poem itself seems to exegete or explicate. The reference at the end of the poem to the "many mansions" of the corncob, which in the prose prelude had only been "empty," furthers the notion of the poem as exegetical commentary on the prose passage while the explicit reference to Christ in the final line of the poem ties together other Biblical references that run throughout the book and also brings to climax the apocalyptic tone that pervades the book.

Everything to which "The eyes are drawn" on "the dusty ground" in the fall of the year, are empty, or broken, or separated from their sources of life:

> pieces of crushed oyster shell
> like doors into the earth made of mother-of-pearl,
> slivers of glass,
> a white chicken's feather that still seems excited
>   by the warm blood,
> and a corncob, all kernals gone, room after room
>   in its endless palace . . . (Bly's ellipsis).

SILENCE IN THE SNOWY FIELDS AND
THIS TREE WILL BE HERE FOR A THOUSAND YEARS

It is in such things that Bly finds a "palace, the place of many mansions, / which Christ has gone to prepare for us." This is "a place to live," as the poem reasserts the statement it comments on. In the world of *This Tree Will Be Here for a Thousand Years* loss is gain and emptiness suggests the presence of the fullness it has displaced.

For all the suggestions of renewal there are in *This Tree*, the dominant tone of the book is dark. The shadow is everywhere and voids and empty places abound. If in *Silence* Bly focused on light and illumination in a landscape of bright, sunlit fields, here the landscape has turned gray and the light become darkened. Nonetheless, the two books, taken together, provide the basis for much of Bly's later work and represent, in the short lyric poem, the dominant mode of his most representative work.

"Out Picking Up Corn" (64, revised in *Selected*, 58), the last poem in *This Tree*, is set in "late December," at the end of the year's cycle. In it Bly writes:

> I am learning; I walk through the plowed fields,
> With a bag, picking up corn for the horses.
> Some small pebbles on the dirt road
> On the way home alight in the late sun.
> Surely we do not eat only with our mouths,
> Or drink only by lifting our hands!
>
> *(Selected* 58)

Clearly, in *Silence* and *This Tree*, Robert Bly is learning the craft of poetry and the strategy and tone of his own most authentic voice for speaking it.

Notes

1. Robert Bly, *Talking All Morning* (Ann Arbor: University of Michigan Press, 1980) 171.

2. Robert Bly, *Silence in the Snowy Fields* (Middletown: Wesleyan University Press, 1962) 29. Reprinted in Bly's *Selected Poems* 10. Hereafter, references to *Silence* and *Selected Poems* will be included in the text.

3. Bly, *Book on the Human Shadow* 7.

4. Bly, *Talking* 131.

5. Howard Nelson, *Robert Bly: An Introduction* 21.

6. Robert Pinsky contends that the first stanza of "Driving . . ." "drifts from uncertainty into boastfulness" and "tells us surprisingly little in a voice of mysterious, bardic hush." (See Pinsky, *The Situation of Poetry: Contemporary Poetry and Its Traditions* [Princeton: Princeton University Press, 1976] 77.)

7. James E. B. Breslin, *From Modern to Contemporary: American Poetry, 1945–1965* (Chicago: University of Chicago Press, 1984) 176–181.

8. Robert Bly, "Some Notes on French Poetry," *The Sixties* 5 (Fall, 1961): 70. Cf. Jerome Rothenberg, another "deep image" poet, who speaks of poetry as "an exploration of the unconscious region of the mind" in which "the unconscious is speaking to the unconscious." (Rothenberg, "Interview," David Ossman, ed. *The Sullen Art* [New York: Corinth Books, 1963] 30–31.)

9. Bly, *Talking* 151.

10. Bly, *Leaping Poetry* 72.

11. Dennis Haskell, "The Modern American Poetry of Deep Image," *Southern Review* (Australia) 12 (1979): 141.

12. Jacob Boehme quoted in Robert Bly, *The Light Around the Body* (New York: Harper & Row, 1967) [1].

13. Robert Bly, "Recognizing the Image as a Form of Intelligence," *Field* 24 (Spring, 1981): 24, 21, 26. Bly revised this essay and retitled it, "What the Image Can Do," (See Donald Hall's *Claims for Poetry* [Ann Arbor: University of Michigan Press, 1982] 38–49.)

14. Lawrence Kramer, "A Sensible Emptiness: Robert Bly and the Poetics of Immanence," *Contemporary Literature* 24:4 (Winter, 1983): 449, 453, 454.

15. Bly has recently revised this poem. See his *Book on the Human Shadow* 18–19 for the revision and Bly's comments on the reasons for it.

16. Bly, *Selected Poems* 12.

17. Philip Dacey, "The Reverend Robert E. Bly, Pastor, Church of the Blessed Unity: A Look at 'A Man Writes to a Part of Himself,' " *Pebble* 18/19/20 (1979): 2. Richard P. Sugg in *Robert Bly* 33, points to a passage in Jung which may have served as one source for Bly's "A Man Writes. . . ." The section in Jung reads: "I was greatly intrigued by the fact that a woman should interfere with me from within. My conclusion was that she must be the 'soul,' in the primitive sense. . . . Then a new idea came to me: in putting down all this material for analysis I was in effect writing letters to the anima, that is, to a part of myself with a different viewpoint from my conscious one." (Jung, *Memories, Dreams, Reflections,* trans. Richard and Clara Winston [New York: Vintage, 1963] 186.)

18. Antonio Machado, *I Never Wanted Fame,* trans. Robert Bly (St. Paul: Ally Press, 1979) viii.

19. Robert Bly, *Sleepers Joining Hands* (New York: Harper & Row, 1973) 59.

20. Bly, *Light* 49.

21. Bly, *Talking* 122–123.

22. Charles Molesworth, "Contemporary Poetry and the Metaphors for the Poem," *Georgia Review* 32:2 (Summer, 1978): 321.

23. Bly, *Book on the Human Shadow* 7–8.

24. Bly, *Talking* 122.

25. Robert Bly, *Old Man Rubbing His Eyes* (Greensboro: Unicorn Press, 1975).

26. Robert Bly, *This Tree Will Be Here for a Thousand Years* (New York: Harper & Row, 1979). Hereafter references to *This Tree* will be included in the text.

27. Bly, "The Two Presences," *This Tree* 11.

28. Bly, *Selected Poems* 27.

29. W. S. Merwin, *The Moving Target* (New York: Atheneum, 1963) 93.

30. Kramer, "Sensible Emptiness" 458.

31. Eliot Weinberger, "Gloves on a Mouse," *The Nation,* 17 November 1979, 504.

32. Hayden Carruth, "Poets on the Fringe," *Harper's,* January 1980, 79.

33. Nelson, *Robert Bly: An Introduction* 187.

34. Kramer, "Sensible Emptiness" 459, 454.

CHAPTER THREE

The Light Around the Body

The contrasts between *Silence in the Snowy Fields* and *The Light Around the Body* are conspicuous, but superficial. Still, the thematic shock of the anti-war poems in the central section of *Light*, taken out of context, can easily divert a reader's attention from the other poems in the book and distort his reading of the complete book. Properly seen, *Light*, like *Silence*, is carefully unified structurally and thematically. And it makes a more powerful poetic statement than it does a political one.

Essentially, both *Silence* and *Light* come from a single source and explore separate sides of the dichotomy which Bly continues to consider primarily in the Boehmean terms of the outward and the inward man, as the passage he uses for his epigraph makes clear:

For according to the outward man, we are in this world, and according to the inward man, we are in the inward world. . . . Since then we are generated

43

out of both worlds, we speak in two languages, and
we must be understood also by two languages.[1]

The first two sections of *Light* define the two
"worlds" in poetic terms. They describe and detail the
translation of an inward world moving outward toward
the explosion which occurs in the third section of the
book. As Bly says in "Watching Television" (6):

> The filaments of the soul slowly separate:
> The spirit breaks, a puff of dust floats up,
> Like a house in Nebraska that suddenly explodes.

The "explosion" of the anti-Vietnam War poems in the
third section, where the outward, political world with
its "various arts of poverty and cruelty" is in control, is
followed by two sections which go back "inward"—first
to "praise grief" and then to the calm of illumination
and transfiguration where "the whole body gives off
light."[2] By structuring his book so carefully and conspicuously surrounding the protest poems with private poems Bly formally stresses the thematic statement of the
book, namely, that outward, public actions and events
have inner, even spiritual, meanings. As Bly has said,
he wrote the poems about the Vietnam War because, he
was "interested in where [the war] came from inside
us";[3] "The truth is that the political poem comes out of
the deepest privacy."[4]

As already mentioned, Bly had been writing protest
poems for many years before *Light* appeared (and indeed, some of the poems in *Light* were written before

many of the poems in *Silence*), but "the Vietnam War and the revulsion against it came down like a rainstorm and carried us away" (*Selected*, 62). The "strange unrest [that] hovers over the nation" even in *Silence* ("Unrest" 25), here, in *Light*, takes specific form and focus.

Light begins with a poem called "The Executive's Death" (3, *Selected* 64). In referring to an anonymous executive Bly might be thinking of Wallace Stevens, the poet and insurance executive from Hartford (mentioned twice in the poem), who was most interested in the theme that Bly's book was about to explore and who had himself explored this same theme in similar terms in his own work. The speaker in Stevens's "Examination of the Hero in a Time of War" begins by saying, "Death is my / Master and, without light, I dwell" but he comes to realize that "the hero is his nation, / In him made one" and that, even in times of war, poetry can redeem the world with "hymns . . . like a stubborn brightness."[5] In accepting the National Book Award for *Light* Bly said, "Our hopes for a life of pure light are breaking up"; and handing over his check to a representative of the draft-resistance movement, he said, "I ask you to use this money . . . to counsel other young men . . . not to destroy their spiritual lives by participating in this war."[6]

"The Busy Man Speaks," the second poem in *Light* (4), is a dramatic monologue which looks back to "A Man Writes to a Part of Himself" in *Silence* and forward to the poems of *The Man in the Black Coat Turns* and *Loving a Woman in Two Worlds*. This busy man lives in a "landscape of zeros," where the mathematics of his money is paralleled with his spiritual emptiness. As Bly says, "The poem reminds us that there are people who make a decision to cut themselves off from the darkness."[7]

The next poem, "Johnson's Cabinet Watched by Ants" (5, *Selected* 69) is interesting in two ways. It provides the first clear indication of the outspoken criticism of the American government and the blatant anti-war poems that follow, but even more interesting is the fact that Bly relates his theme to American literary history as well as American political history. In this way the poem focuses both the literary and historical past on the specific present and thus puts into historical context the immediate concerns of *Light*. Ironically, such a context simultaneously increases the specific, immediate protest of the war in Vietnam at the same time that it encloses it within a historical progression. This is precisely what Bly wants to do. "Johnson's Cabinet Watched by Ants" is only the first of several poems ("After the Industrial Revolution, All Things Happen at Once" and "Hatred of Men with Black Hair," are two of the most obvious) that address these issues in this way.

"Johnson's Cabinet Watched by Ants" begins in "a clearing deep in a forest" at night. Here those "we know during the day . . . appear changed." These lines immediately evoke Hawthorne's "Young Goodman Brown," as Bly has himself recently acknowledged: "The war brought a new corruption of language. The practice of doing ugly things, then describing them in bland words, which Hawthorne wrote of in 'Young Goodman Brown,' thinking of it as a habit of Christian commercial people, became national policy" (*Selected* 63). This reference to Hawthorne, who sets his story in the early Puritan period of the American culture, ties together the beginnings and ends of American history and provides an artistic comment on it. Both Bly and Hawthorne, like Boehme before them, point to the contrast between the dark and light sides of the human psyche, between the outward and inward man:

> Tonight they burn the rice-supplies; tomorrow
> They lecture on Thoreau; tonight they move around the trees,
> Tomorrow they pick the twigs from their clothes;
> Tonight they throw the fire-bombs, tomorrow
> They read the Declaration of Independence; tomorrow they are in church.

The poem ends with the ants, "gathered around an old tree" singing "Old Etruscan songs on tyranny" while, nearby, "toads clap their small hands, and join / The fiery songs." The toads and ants gathered around the old tree, in a metaphoric leap typical of Bly, suggest a communally organized society, easily drawn into "fiery songs."

The first section of *Light* ends with "Romans Angry about the Inner World" (9–10, *Selected* 65) in which the dichotomy between the inner and outer world—here significantly linked with the dichotomy between the masculine and the feminine—is again placed in a historical context and given a historical progression. The reference to the woman being tortured by the Romans, " 'a woman / Who has seen our mother / In the other world!' " ("mother" is capitalized in *Selected*) is a reference to the mystical cult of the Great Mother or Magna Mater that appeared in ancient times: "A late abstraction, presupposing a highly developed speculative consciousness . . . worshipped and portrayed many thousands of years before the appearance of the term"[8] and was finally quashed by the Romans.

This poem anticipates a major theme in Bly which first fully surfaces in *Sleepers Joining Hands*. In his essay in *Sleepers*, "I Came Out of the Mother Naked," Bly proposes that Mother-goddesses suppressed by one culture can return in another, thus the comparison between the American present and ancient Rome.

> The inner world is a thorn
> In the ear of a tiny beast! . . . It is a jagged stone
> Flying toward us out of the darkness. (As revised
>   in *Selected*, 65.)

As Bly says, "America is still young . . . and she may become something magnificent and shining, or she may turn, as Rome did, into a black dinosaur, the enemy of every nation in the world who wants to live its own life."[9]

The next section of *Light* shows "The Various Arts of Poverty and Cruelty." It begins with "Come with Me" (13), an invitation "into those things that have felt this despair for so long," that "howl with a terrible loneliness," that have "black and collapsed bodies . . . those roads in South Dakota that feel around in the darkness . . ." (Bly's ellipsis), where the grief and despair is expressed through places and objects. This is the world of "Those Being Eaten by America" as the next poem defines it and "That is why these poems are so sad" (14). The result of the poverty and cruelty is that, "The world will soon break up into small colonies of the saved" (14).

As prelude to the Vietnam War poems of the central section of *Light* this second section serves primarily as a transition from the inner world to the overt outer world of the war. In this world of "The Great Society" (17):

Dentists continue to water their lawns even in the rain;
Hands developed with terrible labor by apes
Hang from the sleeves of evangelists;
There are murdered kings in the light-bulbs outside movie
   theaters;
The coffins of the poor are hibernating in piles of new tires.
The janitor sits troubled by the boiler,
And the hotel keeper shuffles the cards of insanity.
The President dreams of invading Cuba.

There are several references to Presidents and political history in this section of *Light*. Jefferson, Jackson, Theodore Roosevelt, and Kennedy, as well as "the current administration," are mentioned specifically, several of them more than once. In the collage of real and imagined events from the history of the nation and the speeches of the presidents, Bly suggests the real surrealism that has created "the ideals of America" and "our

freedom to criticize" (25) them which make possible the
blatant anti-war poems that appear in the next section
of the book.

The final poem in this section of the book, "Sleet
Storm on the Merritt Parkway," (25) a poem which
catches up many of Bly's themes in this section and in
Light as a whole, translates the pervasive symbol of
snow from *Silence* to sleet. The Merritt Parkway is a particularly lovely road in southern Connecticut, but Bly is
surely counting on the ironic reverberations of his reference (perhaps especially the obsolete meaning of *merit*
as reward or punishment due) when he contrasts the
"white sleet" with the "black glass," and the "ideals of
America" with the "slave systems of Rome and
Greece." In this world of *Light*, the snow of *Silence*, that
silent, pervasive, positive presence, has been transformed into "the snowy field[s] of the insane asylum"
where children from "the many comfortable homes"
will spend their lives.

The eight poems that make up "The Vietnam War,"
the third section of *Light*, are the poems which the book
has been most criticized for and for which it will be
most conspicuously remembered. The impact of these
poems on a reader is immediate; and they remain the
most specific, the most detailed and the most controversial poetic anti-war statement of the period. They are
what first put Bly in the public eye, and they are, more
than anything else, what keeps him there.

The first poem in this section, "After the Industrial
Revolution, All Things Happen at Once," (29) provides

a convenient transition to the section by linking the contemporary "revolutionary" events surrounding the Vietnam War with the industrial revolution referred to in its
title and with the American Revolution that established
the republic.

Now we enter a strange world, where the Hessian Christmas
Still goes on, and Washington has not reached the other
   shore;
The Whiskey Boys
Are gathering again on the meadows of Pennsylvania
And the Republic is still sailing on the open sea.

Once in this "strange world," Bly moves quickly
and immediately to the contemporary historical setting
of the war in Vietnam and its ramifications in the next
poem, "Asian Peace Offers Rejected without Publication" (30, *Selected* 68). Because "Men like Rusk are not
men only" (as revised in *Selected*) but "bombs waiting to
be loaded in a darkened hangar," the "suggestions by
Asians are not taken seriously," and this outward action
or lack of action by the politicians forces people to try to
find inward reasons for the war. As Bly, again borrow-
ing from the Boehmean dichotomy, said, "I think that
every event has an inward and an outward reason for its
happening. . . . [T]he poems on the war in *The Light
Around the Body* tried to give *inward* reasons for that
war."[10]

In the second stanza of "Asian Peace Offers . . ."
"something inside us / Like a ghost train in the
Rockies / About to be buried in snow" serves as warn-

ing for the disruption of nature and of human nature which the war in Vietnam has created, "Its long hoot / Making the owl in the Douglas fir turn his head . . ." (Bly's ellipsis). This ambiguous gesture of the owl turning his head in attraction or indifference or chagrin suggests the necessity for an outward response to this inner reasoning, and the ellipsis with which the poem ends leaves room for that response—indeed, almost demands it.

Ironically, however, there is no response, as the next poem, "War and Silence" (31, *Selected* 72), makes clear:

> Bishops rush about crying, "There is no war."
> And bombs fall,
> Leaving a dust on the beech trees.
>
> (*Selected* 72)

"Counting Small-Boned Bodies" (32, *Selected* 73) is probably the best-known poem in *Light*, and it is perhaps Bly's most overt castigation of the Vietnam War.

> Let's count the bodies over again.
>
> If we could only make the bodies smaller,
> the size of skulls,
> we could make a whole plain white with skulls in the
>   moonlight.
>
> If we could only make the bodies smaller,
> maybe we could fit
> a whole year's kill in front of us on a desk.

THE LIGHT AROUND THE BODY

> If we could only make the bodies smaller,
> we could fit
> a body into a finger ring, for a keepsake forever.
>
> (*Selected* 73)

Properly understood, "Counting Small-Boned Bodies" fits into the progression of protest that Bly sees as going all the way back to the beginning of American history. As he recently said, "The South Asians, representing a civilization more reconciled to the moist dark than ours, merged with ghostly Cherokees or Crows far down in our psyche. During the Vietnam war we listened every day to brutalizing body tallies, and I felt, and still feel, that the dreamlike quality of the war represented a repetition of some earlier massacres."[11]

"Counting Small-Boned Bodies," of course, refers to the grotesque practice of giving casualty counts nightly on the evening news. The speaker in the poem, one of the keepers of the body count, seems a likeable, mildly perplexed efficiency expert trying, rather ingeniously, to think of ways to do his gruesome job more effectively. Ironically, as he imagines the bodies becoming smaller (a device that allows him to think of them as moving further away), they also get closer to him. The progression from "a whole plain white with skulls in the moonlight" to "a finger ring, for a keepsake forever," is a deft manipulation of perspective and aesthetic distance on Bly's part. The three final stanzas of the poem, each almost identical structurally and syntactically, and each conditional to and dependent upon the first single-

sentence stanza, suggest both structurally and thematically how easy it is for someone to separate himself
from the deaths of his fellow human beings. The dead,
seen only as "bodies" from the outset, become finally
"fit" (a term Bly emphasizes by repeating it in both the
third and fourth stanzas of his revised version) memen-
toes, "keepsakes," to be cherished forever. By the final
line of the poem the circle symbolized by the ring is
complete: the insane logic that allows one to turn people into objects to be counted, can as easily imagine the
possibility of turning objects made out of corpses into
"keepsakes."

In "At a March against the Vietnam War" Bly plays
on the ancient notion of "holy war" and the way that
that notion has been perverted by present society.
Something in the experience of this war touches a chord
deep in man's being: "There are longings to kill that
cannot be seen" (33); "there is something moving in the
dark somewhere / Just beyond / The edge of our eyes"
(34). As a result, "We long to abase ourselves" and carry
around a "cup of darkness" in order that we can "make
war / Like a man anointing himself" (35).

The last two poems in this section of the book, "Hatred of Men with Black Hair" (36, *Selected* 75) and "Driving through Minnesota during the Hanoi Bombings"
(37, *Selected* 74) establish an aesthetic distance between
the outspoken anti-war poems which precede them and
create a transition between these poems and the inward
turning poems which follow them and close the book.
"Hatred of Men with Black Hair," like "After the Indus-

THE LIGHT AROUND THE BODY

trial Revolution, All Things Happen at Once" and "Johnson's Cabinet Watched by Ants," traces other, earlier instances of man's inhumanity to man as a beam of "black light" extending through history. At the end of this poem Bly speaks of the "drop of Indian blood preserved in snow" under the Pentagon, the last remaining drop from "a trail of blood that once led away / . . . the trail now lost" (36). This lost trail of blood is what Bly would seek out, find, and recover, a road toward atonement on both the inner, individual, psychological and the outward, natural, political levels.

In "Driving through Minnesota during the Hanoi Bombings" (37), Bly describes a boy tortured with a telephone generator. This scene parallels the scene of the woman being tortured on the iron horse in "Romans Angry about the Inner World" (9), the last poem in the first section of the book. The difference between these poems is that the hint of reconciliation in the earlier poem is here made much more explicit and much more personal as Bly stresses the inward-outward dichotomy he is so obsessed with and as he explores the need for inward reasons for outward actions.

In this regard Bly is not alone. In trying to define the essence of the poetry written during the 1960s, "the new contemporary poem," Paul Breslin stresses the relationship between psychology and politics so important to Bly and to many other poets in this period. This "New Left" finds the basis for its political theory in the writings of Herbert Marcuse, Paul Goodman, Norman O. Brown, and R. D. Laing, all of whose work was "*psycho*-political in emphasis. These thinkers, and those who make use of them, believe that in the apparently free society of a Western democracy, political oppression occurs primarily through psychological conditioning rather than coercive force" and that, "The recovery of the repressed through the exploration of one's own psyche was inextricably bound up with any real political change."[12]

In "Driving through Minnesota during the Hanoi Bombings" the poet has returned home, back to the "silence in the snowy fields," and he has returned a changed man. The outward events of the war and its atrocities have seeped into the speaker's consciousness and into his own personal psychic landscape in such a way that he realizes that the ultimate destruction and havoc wrought by the war in Vietnam has been to the psyche of the inner man ("We were the ones we intended to bomb!") and that the only real means of atonement available to right this wrong must find its source in an inner reconciliation of man to himself. Once this personal healing process has begun, and only then, can man hope to heal the world in which he lives.

The "grief" that Bly felt "the day we bombed Hanoi for the first time,"[13] the day "Driving through Minnesota during the Hanoi Bombings" was written, must work on the "instants" of the war "become crystals, / Particles / The grass cannot dissolve" and "Therefore we will have / To go far away / To atone / For the sufferings" (37) inflicted on Vietnam. According to Bly, "the poets see the issue more clearly . . . than the politicians" and therefore they must write poetry which will "do something revolutionary both in language and in politics."[14] That "something revolutionary" will never again be so explicit in Bly's work as it has been in this central section of *Light*, but it will always be there, under the surface of even his most mild poems.

As the first two sections of *Light* move outward from an inner world, so the two final sections move back inward, after the outward world of the anti-war poems in the middle section. Bly has said, "The exaggerations on both sides damaged the language of public debate in the United States. By the end of the war, I felt some affinity gone in me, and I wanted to return to privacy rather than to go on judging" (*Selected* 63).

The first step in this return to privacy is to feel grief. The first poem in the fourth section is "Melancholia" (41), a poem which immediately evokes the world of *Silence in the Snowy Fields*. "Turning Away from Lies," the next poem, asks, "When shall I have peace?" (43).

The third poem, "A Home in Dark Grass" (44, *Selected* 16), makes an important thematic statement for the book as a whole—indeed it makes an important thematic statement for the whole of Bly's work, as is indicated by the fact, first of all, that he has revised it extensively for his *Selected Poems* (16) and that, in the *Selected Poems*, he placed it in the early section of the book, entitled "The Road of Poverty and Death."

The title, "A Home in Dark Grass," is full of value words for Bly, and the first line, "In the deep fall, the body awakes" (44), stresses several of his dominant themes: the awakening of the body is seen as part of the natural cycle of the season's or the year's turning, the awakening of the body to its own inwardness. This metaphor of the body awakening (the dominant theme of the final section of *Light*) is described here in terms of both rebirth and atonement and, although described in the context of natural progressions, there are obvious theological overtones which suggest the mystique of man's relationship with nature, the way man's nature and nature herself seem to strive toward similar goals: "The wind rises, the water is born, / Spreading white tomb-clothes on a rocky shore, / Drawing us up / From the bed of the land (44).

The crucial second stanza has been significantly revised by Bly. His theme can perhaps best be seen by comparing the two versions:

> We did not come to remain whole.
> We came to lose our leaves like the trees,
> The trees that are broken
> And start again, drawing up from the great roots;
> Like mad poets captured by the Moors,
> Men who live out
> A second life.
>
> (*Light*, 44)

* * *

> It is not our job to remain unbroken.
> Our task is to lose our leaves
> And be born again, as trees
> Draw up from the great roots.
> So men captured by the Moors

THE LIGHT AROUND THE BODY

> Wake in the detached ocean
> Air, living a second life.
>
> *(Selected, 16)*

The first version stresses, in both word choice and rhetoric, an almost Biblical description of man's condition and his necessary and appropriate action in the world. The "great roots" suggest a source of inwardness within man which, even though his outward body is broken (indeed even because it ought to be: "We came to lose . . .") can "start again" by "drawing up from the great roots" and thus allow a man to live a "second life." The revision changes the tone slightly through the use of words like "job" and "task" and more clearly focuses the last three lines, where "mad poets" become simply "men" who "wake" to a second life. But the main thematic thrust of the poem remains constant as the value words of the title are restressed in the final three lines of the poem—which Bly did not change:

> And, dancing, find in the trees a savior,
> A home in dark grass,
> And nourishment in death.
>
> *(44, Selected 16)*

"A Home in Dark Grass" is Bly's clearest expression of his dominant theme.[15]

As already mentioned (see chapter two), "The Fire of Despair Has Been Our Saviour" is one of Bly's earliest poems. In its earliest version, as "The Man Who Sees the Hill of Despair from Afar," Bly included it in his 1956 M.A. thesis. He has further revised the version here in *Light* (48–49) and included it in his *Selected Poems* (14). In *Talking,* after acknowledging the already long history of the poem, Bly said, "In desperation, I put it into *The Light Around the Body.* I had worked on it ten years. . . . I'll do it again. I thought it was all right when I published it, but it isn't. I mean that the sensation of grief is very important in finding the road."[16] In short, the theme of this poem has been, and remains, an important theme for Bly. Certainly, it is one of the most important poems in *Light.*

The title, "The Fire of Despair Has Been Our Saviour," immediately suggests the possibility of hope through the cleansing fire of hopelessness, or the possibility of salvation through despair. This is very much in keeping with the Danish philosopher Søren Kierkegaard's thinking. Indeed, Kierkegaard has been an important, if unnoticed, influence on Bly from the beginning. (Bly first read Kierkegaard closely in the 1950s.) Kierkegaard calls despair "the sickness unto death" and says that "the dying of despair transforms itself constantly into a living."[17] And the whole thrust of this section of *Light*, "In Praise of Grief," is to make possible this kind of paradoxical Kierkegaardian transformation/resurrection. As Bly has said, if a poem "moves into deep and painful regions of the memory" it is "sometimes able to be a kind of atonement."[18]

"The Fire of Despair Has Been Our Saviour" begins in autumn. The trees, "Heaven's roots," are bare but "holy" because, in them, "How easily we see spring coming," even if there seems to be no reason for seeing a similar rebirth in man. The speaker in "This [same] autumn . . . / Cannot find the road / . . . the things that we must grasp, / The signs, are gone . . ." (48). He thinks back through history, first to the Middle Ages (a pun is intended), "iron ringing iron," and then further back, to the Ice Age, where "in agony / Man cried out— like the mad hog, pierced, again, / Again by teeth- spears, who / Grew his horny scales / From sheer despair" but which created "instants / Finally leading out of the snowbound valley!" (48). In short, through- out history "the fire of despair has been our saviour" and the speaker, having made his brief historical survey, raises the question about the present time: "Where has the road gone?" He seems to be unable to find in the present any trace of redemption or hope through de- spair:

All
Trace lost, like a ship sinking,
Where what is left and what goes down both bring
    despair.
Not finding the road, we are slowly pulled down. (49)

Perhaps this conclusion is not as negative as it first seems. The ship sinks, and "what is left and what goes down" simply submerge into the psyche in order that they can be brought up or out from it again. Thus the being "pulled down" is only the prelude to being raised back up again, as Kierkegaard suggests, or as Bly's own theories yet to come (but already formulated) suggest. All of this is more clearly expressed in the latest version of the poem: "I sink and don't sink" (*Selected*, 14). Surely, the continuing vision of this poem—which stretches from his earliest beginnings to his most recent revisions—needs to be kept in mind in reading the complete Bly.

The final section of *Light*, "A Body Not Yet Born," is just that, a body not yet born but in process or in progress toward birth. The poems in this section, as the title of one of them, "Moving Inward at Last" (57), suggests, are the most "inward" of all of the poems of *Light*. The contrast between the earlier "outward" poems and these "inward" ones is amazing—incredible unless one understands what Bly is trying to do both thematically and structurally in this book.

"Looking into a Face" (53) is the poem from which both this section and the book take their titles.

> Conversation brings us so close! Opening
> The surfs of the body,
> Bringing fish up near the sun,
> And stiffening the backbones of the sea!
>
> I have wandered in a face, for hours,
> Passing through dark fires.
> I have risen to a body
> Not yet born,
> Existing like a light around the body,
> Through which the body moves like a sliding moon.

As Bly said in "Late at Night During a Visit of Friends" (*Silence*, 58), "The human face shines as it speaks of things / Near itself, thoughts full of dreams. /

THE LIGHT AROUND THE BODY

The human face shines like a dark sky." Ultimately, "Looking into a Face" combines many of Bly's most overt themes, not only in *Light* but in his poetry in general. As it is expressed in this poem, through what has by now become a paradox basic to Bly's work, the outward man, via a series of "leaps" that open "the surfs of the body," moves "inward at last" in order to rise "to a body not yet born," the "perfect body" which Norman O. Brown speaks of, a "body reconciled with death."[19]

The presence of the body "risen to" but "not yet born" can be defined only in terms of the absence of presence, which "exist[s] like a light around the body, / Through which the body moves like a sliding moon." That which will be "risen to" is that which has always already existed invisibly before, like "light around the body," but which will be realized only when visibly "seen" through the presence of its absence. Bly thinks of this in terms of his notion of the "third brain" or the "new brain" which he borrows primarily from the work of Paul MacLean. (This idea and its significance for Bly's thought and poetry will be considered below.) The "new brain" contains much of man's spiritual energy and can create a situation in which "the whole body gives off light," as in the transfiguration or in the "stories of old Tibetan meditators who sit in a room reading a book by the light of their own bodies." This is, Bly acknowledges, something "we have never understood . . . well."[20]

Apocalyptic or eschatological images are frequent in the final section of *Light*. In "The Hermit" (55) Bly writes of "a man whose body is perfectly whole" and although "He is no one. When we see / Him, we grow calm / And sail on into the tunnels of joyful death." In "Evolution from the Fish" (59) "This nephew of snails" whose "head throws off light" is "moving toward his own life / Like fur, walking . . . / . . . dragging a great tail into the darkness." In "Wanting to Experience All Things" (60) there is "a paw / [that] Comes out of the dark / To light the road," and "fiery traces through the night!" (60).

"Moving Inward at Last" (57) is one of the most important poems in this section. It points to a movement "inward," the direction that both this book and most of Bly's remaining work will take. Further, it describes this psychological movement in theological metaphors and thus climaxes the dominant thematic movement of *Light*.

"Moving Inward at Last" opens with the evocation of a religious sacrifice on a mountain altar. But the sacrifice of the dying bull seems not to have effected any changes. Things "inside the mountain . . . antlers, bits of oak bark, / Fire, herbs," are "untouched / By the blood" of the sacrifice. Even so, from inside a cave in the mountain, a transformation is about to take place:

> When the smoke touches the roof of the cave,
> The green leaves burst into flame,
> The air of night changes to dark water,
> The mountains alter and become the sea.

The sacrifice in the exterior, outward world, on the mountaintop, fails, but the inward changes succeed.

THE LIGHT AROUND THE BODY

Punning on the contrast between the mountain altar
and the "mountains alter[ing]," Bly stresses the necessity of changing the outward world by working from
within. The mountains, like the air changed to water,
are submerged in the sea.

 Light ends with "When the Dumb Speak," (62, *Selected* 15) with "The body raging / And driving itself,
disappearing in smoke."

> Then images appear:
> Images of death,
> Images of the body shaken in the grave,
> And the graves filled with seawater;
> Fires in the sea,
> The ships smoldering like bodies,
> Images of wasted life,
> Life lost, imagination ruined,
> The house fallen,
> The gold sticks broken,
> Then shall the talkative be silent,
> And the dumb speak. (62)

Although at first this seems negative, ultimately it must
be seen as a rather strong affirmation in the same way
that *Light* must be seen as positive and affirmative. The
"dumb" who "shall speak," who *do* speak here at the
end of poem and book, are both the dead in Vietnam
whose voice has been their deeds and the long dead
who still live in the psyches of the living and who, although they may have been asleep, are, in terms of the
metaphor of Bly's next book, about to awaken and "join
hands."[21]

Notes

1. Jacob Boehme quoted in Robert Bly, *The Light Around the Body* (New York: Harper & Row, 1967) [1]. Hereafter, references to *Light* will be included in the text.

2. Bly, *Talking* 43.

3. Bly, *Talking* 83.

4. Bly, "Leaping Up into Political Poetry," 11.

5. Wallace Stevens, *The Collected Poems* (New York: Random House, 1982) 273, 279.

6. Robert Bly, "Acceptance of the National Book Award for Poetry, March 6, 1968," *Tennessee Poetry Journal* 2:2 (Winter, 1969): 14–15.

7. Bly, *Book on the Human Shadow* 10.

8. Erich Neumann, *The Great Mother: An Analysis of the Archetype,* trans. Ralph Manheim (Princeton: Princeton University Press, 1972) 11.

9. Bly, "Leaping Up into Political Poetry," 17. In *A Poetry Reading Against the Vietnam War* (7) Bly notes that, in 1966, the Marine Corps made comparisons between Rome and present-day America.

10. Bly, *Talking* 154–155.

11. Bly, *Book on the Human Shadow* 11.

12. Paul Breslin, "How to Read the New Contemporary Poem," *The American Scholar* 47:3 (Summer, 1978): 365.

13. Bly, *Talking* 88.

14. Bly, *Talking* 59, 154.

15. For a somewhat different, but very interesting analysis of "A Home in Dark Grass," see Charles Altieri, *Enlarging the Temple: New Directions in American Poetry during the 1960's* (Lewisburg: Bucknell University Press, 1979) 88–90.

16. Bly, *Talking* 124.

17. Søren Kierkegaard, *The Sickness Unto Death* in *A Kierkegaard Anthology,* ed. Robert Bretall (New York: Random House, n.d.) 341–342.

18. Robert Bly, "The Collapse of James Dickey," *The Sixties* 9 (Spring, 1967): 70.

19. Norman O. Brown, *Life Against Death* (Middletown: Wesleyan University Press, 1959) 308–309.

20. Bly, *Talking* 43.

21. For a more detailed analysis of Bly's political poetry in the early part of his career, and of *Light* in particular, see Davis's " 'Hair in a Baboon's Ear': The Politics of Robert Bly's Early Poetry," *The Carleton Miscellany* 18:1 (Winter, 1979–80): 74–84.

CHAPTER FOUR

Sleepers Joining Hands

S*leepers Joining Hands* (1973) is a transitional book and it is a book in transition. It is transitional in that Bly synthesizes the dominant themes and styles of *Silence* and *Light* in preparation for work that is to come. It is a book in transition in that Bly has reworked its material, particularly the long title poem, for many years—and continues to rework it. Thus, if *Sleepers* does not contain Bly's most important poetry, it contains much of the major theoretical material which makes possible an accurate reading of his most important poetry.

Sleepers is made up of three sections, the first and last poetry, the seminal central section an essay in prose. The first section is further subdivided into two parts which thematically and stylistically parallel Bly's first two books, *Silence* and *Light*, while the final long title poem in the third section points out the further direction his work will take. As such, *Sleepers* flashes forward to poems yet to come and back over poems already written and illuminates major themes and dominant stylistic modes.

The book begins with "Six Winter Privacy Poems."[1] The first of these clearly harks back to *Silence:*

> About four, a few flakes.
> I empty the teapot out in the snow
>   feeling shoots of joy in the new cold.
> By nightfall, wind,
> the curtains on the south sway softly.

By the sixth of these little poems, along with the "new snow," "someone else," a specter of what is to come, has been introduced, following an "awakening."

> When I woke, new snow had fallen.
> I am alone, yet someone else is with me,
> drinking coffee, looking out at the snow.

Between the moments of these two stanzas Bly mentions his shack of "two rooms," of "fly[ing] into one of my own poems," the dying of the "fathers," the "darkness [that] appears as flakes of light," a religious music, and a "joy" that has its source either in "the body, or the soul, or a third place." In short, these little poems are a microcosm of Bly's early poetic world, particularly the world of *Silence.*

Several of the other short poems in this first section of *Sleepers* deserve some attention. "Water Under the Earth" (6–7, revised and retitled "Chinese Tomb Guardians" in *Selected* 126–127), which Bly calls the "book of

my confessions" in the first line, is clearly a key poem.
In many ways it parallels the whole of *Sleepers,* and it
specifically anticipates the long title poem of the third
section of the book.

The title, "Water Under the Earth," suggests something submerged which needs to be tapped and
brought up to the surface—in direct opposition to the
commandment in Exodus 20:4 from which the poem
takes its title. ("You shall not make for yourself a graven
image, or any likeness of anything that is in heaven
above, or that is in the earth beneath or that is in the
water under the earth.") As will soon be seen, this need
to allow things to surface is, psychologically, exactly
what Bly believes it is necessary for man to do if he is to
realize his greatest potential, and it is precisely what
Bly, in his poems from this point on, has attempted to
do. When "what was swallowed, pushed away,
sunken / . . . begins to rise" (*Selected* 126), then the new
direction can be glimpsed even though the poet recognizes that:

> I am less than half risen. I see how carefully
> I have covered my tracks as I wrote,
> how well I have brushed over the past with my tail.
> (*Selected* 126)

Bly seems to be alluding here to the contrast between
his early poems which do not "leap" enough compared
to the poems of "ancient times," the " 'time of inspiration,' " when poets "flew from one world to another
'riding on dragons,' " and "dragged behind them long

tails of dragon smoke" which meant "that a leap has taken place in the poem." It is this "leap to the unknown part of the mind" that "lies in the very center" of "all art derived from Great Mother mysteries,"[2] which is the kind of poetry Bly now wants to write, the kind of poetry typified by "dragon smoke."

> Faces look at me from the shallow waters,
> where I have pushed them down—
> father and mother pushed into the dark.
> (*Selected* 126)

The "father and mother" here suggest the mother and father consciousness Bly develops later in the book and also points toward later books, especially *The Man in the Black Coat Turns* and *Loving a Woman in Two Worlds*. The speaker of this poem, standing "at the edges of the light" aware of the "consciousness hovering under the mind's feet" (7) is finally described as "a father who dips as he passes over underground rivers, / who can feel his children through all distance and time!" (7). He is, in short, a link between past and future.

"Hair" (10–12, revised as "A Conversation" 119–121, and "Aban Kavost and Ivar Oakeson" 122 in *Selected*) is very much a "leaping" poem. It seems to be set in an ancient time and many of the images are surreal: "Thousands and thousands of years go by, / like an infinite procession of walnut shells"; "the hair weeps, / because hair does not long for immense states"; "Nailheads that have been brooding on Burton's *Melancholy* under Baltimore rowhouses / roll out in the street, underneath tires, / and catch the Secretary of State / as he goes off to threaten the premiers of underdeveloped nations." This "hair is overflowing with excitable children"; it "carries the holy, shouting to the other shore." And "Under the ground the earth has hair cathedrals"; "the priest comes down the aisle wearing caterpillar fur" (10–12).

In the poems into which "Hair" is divided in *Selected* the conversational exchange is emphasized. "A Conversation" is divided into four alternating parts, two each headed "Judgment" and "Affinity." "Aban Kavost and Ivar Oakeson," is a continuation of the conversation of the first poem, and the new material Bly has added in it makes much more clear what was, all along, somewhat hidden in "Hair."[3] Looked at closely the poem and its revisions contains, implicitly, much of the theory and imagery that Bly will develop explicitly in his essay, "I Came Out of the Mother Naked," in the middle of *Sleepers*, which, in turn, becomes the basis for the rest of his work, in this book and beyond.

The significance of the doppelgänger (literally a "double-goer") figure Aban Kavost-Ivar Oakeson is made clear in their final exchange:

> *Aban K.* I suffered for years and you remained in ease!
> I am the strong one; I have endured pain.
> I suffer and do while you go into ecstasy.
> Women love you, not me; and I raged at the start
> from my carrying you. No more. I will blind you.
> *Ivar O.* Have you put bonds on me? Are you that strong?
> (*Selected* 122)

This doubling is further detailed in another largely new poem, "The Man Locked Inside the Oak" (*Selected* 125):

> One man in me is locked inside an oakwomb,
>
> . . . .
>
> Who is the man locked inside the oakwomb?
> A dangerous man; and there is the grief man,
> Ivar Oakeson, whom I love so much.
> Others false and ghostly live within me also.

The first section of *Sleepers* concludes with "The Teeth Mother Naked at Last" (18–26), the longest and the most important of Bly's anti-war poems, which Joyce Carol Oates calls a "small masterpiece . . . which will probably be remembered as the finest poem to have grown out of the antiwar movement of the Sixties."[4]

"Teeth Mother" exists in three versions: the original version published by City Lights Books in 1970; the somewhat different version included in *Sleepers* in 1973; the revision of the *Sleepers* version published in *Selected* in 1986. For the sake of convenience and because it is Bly's final version of the poem, the *Selected* (76–86) text will be used as the basis for this discussion.

In his preface to *A Poetry Reading Against the Vietnam War* Bly suggests the theme of "Teeth Mother" when he says that the "really serious evil of the war, rarely discussed, is the harm it will do the American inwardly."[5] It is for this very reason, to help alleviate the inward harm of the war in Vietnam, that Bly writes "Teeth Mother."

"Teeth Mother," like many of the anti-war poems in *Light*, is didactic and controversial, propagandistic and surreal, but it is also a political, social, and psychological analysis of the malaise of modern society for which the war in Vietnam is only the most immediate and obvious example. In responding subjectively and poetically to the war, in parodying the political propaganda it created, and in tracing its sources through the depths of man's psyche, Bly hopes to awaken himself and his reader to understanding and therapeutic action.

"Teeth Mother" is divided into seven numbered, self-contained sections and is written in what Bly calls "the Smart-Blake-Whitman line," a line "which is flung out from the left-hand wall . . . unsupported by interlocking syntax at the further end, yet remains aloft, alert, long-winded, holding its energy, airy as a hawk's wing." It is a line which, in general, belongs to "declaration rather than inquiry, to prophecy rather than meditation, to public speech rather than inner debate,"[6] although Bly wishes to stress equally both elements of each of these dichotomies. The figure of the Teeth Mother who appears at the end of the poem is a figure drawn from Bly's study of the mother archetype in Jung and Neumann (which he treats in detail in the prose section, "I Came Out of the Mother Naked," immediately following "Teeth Mother"). The poem also sets up two important themes to come: the "sleepers joining hands" metaphor which gives the book its title ("It is the longing for someone to come and take us by the hand to where they all are sleeping," 81); and the theory of the three brains which figures significantly in the long title poem at the end of *Sleepers* ("I would suddenly go back to my animal brain" 85).

The "terrible beauty" born of the war is immediately evoked at the outset of "Teeth Mother" as the "Massive engines lift beautifully" from the decks of aircraft carriers and "sweep over the huts with dirt floors" (*Selected* 76). This "death-bee" of economic origin is "Hamilton's triumph . . . the triumph of a centralized bank" that makes "the hopes of Tolstoy fall asleep in the ant heap. . . . / Now the time comes to look into the past-tunnels" (76). The dying know "the mansions of the dead are empty," rooms and children "explode" in a fiery apocalypse, and "Blood leaps on the vegetable walls" (77).

The central sections of the poem document the hypocrisies and lies which are used to defend the war. They are attempts to analyze what these lies mean from a psychological point of view.

> Now the Chief Executive enters, and the press conference
>   begins.
> First the President lies about the date the Appalachian
>   Mountains rose.
> Then he lies about the population of Chicago,
> then the weight of the adult eagle, and the acreage of the
>   Everglades.
> Next he lies about the number of fish taken every year in
>   the Artic.

He has private information about which city *is* the capital
   of Wyoming.
He lies next about the birthplace of Attila the Hun,
Then about the composition of the amniotic fluid.

He insists that Luther was never a German,
and only the Protestants sold indulgences.
He declares that Pope Leo X *wanted* to reform the Church,
   but the liberal elements prevented him.
He declares the Peasants' War was fomented by Italians
   from the North.
And the Attorney General lies about the time the sun
   sets.

These lies mean that something in the nation wants to
   die.

(*Selected* 80)[7]

   The question asked, over and over again, is, "Why
are they dying?" (84). The answer lies buried in the psychological makeup of men who, when they gain wealth
and prosperity, when "the culture of affluence opens
the psyche to the Teeth Mother," as Bly says in his essay
(43), find that they simultaneously seek to expiate the
guilt they have accumulated along the road to prosperity by attempting to destroy that more primitive culture
from which they themselves came and which serves as
a constant reminder of a past they hope they have oblit-
erated, a past whose presence must be destroyed if the
future they envision is to become a reality.
   But even if this is so, it does not decrease the terror,

which increases as the poem moves from the general to
the particular, from the third person to the first:

> But if one of those children came near that we have set
>   on fire,
> came toward you like a gray barn, walking,
> you would howl like a wind tunnel in a hurricane,
> you would tear at your shirt with blue hands,
> you would drive over your own child's wagon trying to
>   back up,
> the pupils of your eyes would go wild.
>
> . . . .
>
> If one of those children came toward me with both hands
> in the air, fire rising along both elbows,
> I would suddenly go back to my animal brain,
> I would drop on all fours screaming;
> my vocal cords would turn blue; so would yours.
> It would be two days before I could play with one of my
>   own children again.
>
> (Selected 84–85)

After this terrifying vision of the war's atrocities
committed even against innocent children, the poem
moves quickly to its apocalyptic close with the evocation of the Teeth Mother herself rising up from waters
both literal and psychological (cf. "Water Under the
Earth" and "Water Drawn Up Into the Head," the "companion poems" in the first and last sections of the
book). The Teeth Mother seems to surface from dream
("I want to sleep awhile. . . . Don't wake me." [85]) and

her presence, "naked at last," results in one vivid final
passage:

> Let us drive cars
> up
> the light beams
> to the stars . . .
>
> And return to earth
> and live inside the drop of sweat
> that falls from the chin of the Protestant tied in the fire.
>
> (*Selected* 86)

These images are as intriguing as any in Bly's work.
The idea of driving cars up light beams suggests modern technology, in both its constructive and destructive
forms, following its own "lights," ironically moving
through itself (the car overtaking the light it follows)
and advancing toward the source (the stars) of self (matter, the universe). Following the fade-out of the ellipsis
there is the necessary "return to earth," the inevitable
completion of the natural cycle. The image of the "drop
of sweat" falling back to earth from the heavens as simultaneously being a drop of sweat falling from the
chin of a martyr being burned for his beliefs, makes for
a surreal juxtaposition of the mundane and the extraordinary, the finite and the infinite, the earthy and the
ethereal. And in this death there is life. Indeed, the
only way life can revive is through death. "Teeth
Mother" then, points to the possibility of both a political and a psychic renewal.

The theory that "Teeth Mother" exemplifies is discussed in the long essay, "I Came Out of the Mother

Naked," which follows it and makes up the central section of *Sleepers.*

"I Came Out of the Mother Naked" has been
viewed in several ways. To some it is Bly's most specific
and detailed summary of his thinking on mother and
father consciousness, Jungian psychology and the archetypes, as well as the idea of the tripartite "new
brain"; to others it is only "a shuffling interlude of notions on parade."[8] Even though Bly himself admits that
the essay "is full of mad generalizations,"[9] it is extremely important to an understanding of much of Bly's
work and of *Sleepers* in specific. As Howard Nelson
says, "Even a reader who begins with a basic skepticism
toward" it "is likely to emerge . . . feeling that he has
been given a rich and useful set of metaphors"[10] with
which to interpret Bly's work.

Bly tries to suggest the universality of the ideas he
is about to detail in his essay by beginning with epigraphs from the *Tao Te Ching,* representing Eastern traditions, and from the Old Testament, representing
Western traditions. Even here at the outset, however, it
is clear that Bly intends to put his own interpretation on
these references, traditions, and ideas. In the well-
known passage from Job 1:21, Job says, "Naked came I
out of my mother's womb, and naked shall I return
thither: the Lord gave and the Lord hath taken away;
blessed be the name of the Lord." Bly renders this passage this way:

> *I came out of the Mother naked,*
> *and I will be naked when I return.*

> *The Mother gave, and the Mother takes away,*
> *I love the Mother.*
> Old Testament, *restored*
> (*Sleepers* 27)[11]

The essay proper is divided into eight numbered sections. Bly rather systematically details the historical tradition of mother consciousness which begins with Johann Bachofen's *Mother Right* (1861) and continues in Jung and Erich Neumann. Bachofen showed that "in every past society known a matriarchy has preceded the present patriarchy. . . . Because men prefer not to remember the thousands and thousands of years in which the Great Mother had total power, almost no one has discussed what we could call 'the Change.' " Still, "knowledge denied to the conscious mind for several thousand years seeps up." Therefore, "We have then inside us two worlds of consciousness: one world associated with the dark, and one world with the light. . . . The dark half corresponds to the consciousness developed in the matriarchies, the white to the consciousness developed in the patriarchies that followed." Matriarchal thinking "is intuitive and moves by associative leaps," is "interested primarily in what is inside walls," has "affection for nature, compassion, love of water, grief and care for the dead, love of whatever is hidden, intuitive, ecstasy." In contrast, "Patriarchies become aware of the space between walls," create empires, and try "to reach the spirit through asceticism" (29–32).

SLEEPERS JOINING HANDS

Four different mothers, "a union of four 'force fields' " (43), make up the Great Mother: the Good Mother, "who brings to birth and nourishes what is born," and who "wants everything now alive to remain alive" (34); the Death Mother, whose "job is to end everything the Good Mother has brought to birth" (37); the Dancing or Ecstatic Mother, who "tends to intensify mental and spiritual life until it reaches ecstasy" (39) and is the source of all poetry; and the Stone or Teeth Mother, who destroys "the intensification of mental life" and "ecstasy and spiritual growth," and who "stands for numbness, paralysis, catatonia . . . the end of psychic life, the dismembering of the psyche" (41–42).

At the end of his essay Bly says:

The increasing strength of poetry, defense of earth, and mother consciousness, implies that after hundreds of years of being motionless, the Great Mother is moving again in the psyche. Every day her face becomes clearer. We are becoming more sensitive, more open to her influence. She is returning, or we are returning to her; everyone who looks down into his own psyche sees her, just as in leaves floating on a pond you can sometimes make out faces. The pendulum is just now turning away from the high point of father consciousness and starting to sweep down. The pendulum rushes down, the Mothers rush toward us, we can all feel the motion downward, the speed increasing. (48)

And although Bly says, "I don't expect these ideas to help writers write better poems," (48) he also says, "I see in my own poems and the poems of so many other poets alive now fundamental attempts to right our . . . spiritual balance" (50).

The outgrowth of Bly's thinking in "I Came Out of the Mother Naked" is clearly, immediately, evident in "Sleepers Joining Hands," the long title poem in four parts which concludes the book.

If "Sleepers Joining Hands" is "Bly's most challenging and most beautiful poem to date,"[12] it is not surprising that it has received substantial and diverse criticism. It has been explicated as "fundamentally and formally psychological . . . with an implicit and continuous parallelism to Jung's schema"[13]; as a "dream journal . . . slipping back and forth across the border of sleep"[14]; and as "Bly's psychospiritual, Jungian epic . . . describing the quest to achieve selfhood" that becomes "a veritable theodicy for the twentieth century."[15]

"Sleepers Joining Hands," Bly's title, is intriguing. In 1959 Denise Levertov, a poet Bly knew and respected, wrote a "testament" in which she said, "I long for poems of an inner harmony in utter contrast to the chaos in which they exist. Insofar as poetry has a social function it is to awaken sleepers by other means than shock." In 1973 Levertov added an interpretative "postscript" to her earlier statement. She said, "I was deploring shock as an end in itself, while espousing the act of 'awakening sleepers' as a goal (not *the* goal) proper to poetry."[16] It may be that this metaphor of the sleepers

has been passed back and forth reciprocally between
the two poets over the years.

The version of the poem in *Sleepers* is a condensa-
tion and revision of a much longer version of either
5,000 or 10,000 lines[17] which Bly says were "written by
some other part of me."[18] And this 480-line version in
Sleepers has been further rewritten into new poems,
"some in minor detail, others in a larger way" in the
Selected Poems (114).[19] The original "radical or root
poem" (*Selected* 114) as it appears in *Sleepers* will be the
basis of the discussion here.

"Sleepers Joining Hands" shifts back and forth between dream and waking reality, between conscious
and unconscious "states of mind," and this accounts for
the structure as well as the way the filaments and
threads of the theme weave their ways through the
poem. The poem itself exists on the edge of sleep, half
in the conscious, half in the unconscious, half "awake,"
half "asleep." In consequence, private myth often gets
interpreted in terms of public myth and dream reality
often supersedes waking reality.

"The Shadow Goes Away" (53–55, revised to "A
Dream of a Brother" [115] and "The Woman Bewil-
dered" [124] in *Selected*) is the first poem in "Sleepers."
Bly says that he began this poem "with images suggesting Joseph's betrayal of his brother" because he imagined his childhood "by imagining two personalities,
one of whom had betrayed the other" (*Selected* 114).
This betrayal, based initially on a Biblical text, is related,
through dream, to the loss of the shadow in a psycho-

logical, Jungian, context and to a specifically American, almost mythological, context when the brother given "to the dark people passing" is "taken in by traveling Sioux" (53).

The concept of the shadow as the "negative side" of the personality, an "unconscious personality," is basic to Jungian thought. For Jung, recognizing the shadow, which represents the personal unconscious, and is the most accessible of the archetypes, is "the essential condition for any kind of self-knowledge."[20] Jung says, "The conscious mind is on top, the shadow underneath, and all consciousness . . . seeks its unconscious opposite. . . . The shadow personifies everything that the subject refuses to acknowledge about himself and yet is always thrusting itself upon him directly or indirectly. . . ."[21] Responding to these notions, Bly asks, "How did the two persons get separated?" and suggests that "We spend the first twenty-five years of life deciding what should be pushed down into the shadow self, and the next forty years trying to get in touch with that material again." Since "cultures vary a lot in what they urge their members to exile," we can say that "in general . . . 'the shadow' represents all that is instinctive in us."[22]

The poem describes how:

> Men bound my shadow. That was in high school.
> They tied it to a tree, I saw it being led away. . . .
> I was alone, asleep in the Law. (54)

As Jung says, "Western man is in danger of losing his shadow altogether, of identifying himself with his fic-

tive personality and the world with the abstract picture
painted by scientific rationalism."[23] Keeping the trappings of the Joseph story, Bly describes the separate
sides of the self in terms of brothers, here almost in
terms of Joseph Conrad's ("a great master of shadow
literature")[24] "The Secret Sharer": "I slipped off one
night into the water, swam to shore with no one watching, / left my brother alone on the ship!" (54). (In *Selected* these lines read, "I took my brother to the other
side of the river, / then swam back, left my brother
alone on the shore" [115], which emphasizes the
"stream" of consciousness and removes the societal setting of the ship. Clearly, Bly continues to explore his
thinking and to revise his poems in terms of that exploration.)[25]

"The Shadow Goes Away" then is a kind of dream
journal. The shadow, which as Jung indicates is often
personified in a dream, appears as the several brother
figures in the poem. The speaker, who has earlier defined himself in terms of family, organized religion, and
the law, experiences, through this dream, a night journey that simultaneously shows him the shadow he has
lost or repressed and, at the same time, implies the
need to regain that shadowy brother-self.

At the outset of "Meeting the Man Who Warns Me"
(56–58, revised as "Night Frogs" 116, and "Falling
Asleep" 117, in *Selected*) the poet awakens and finds
himself "in the woods, far from the castle" (56, *Selected*
116). "A woman whispers to me, urges me to speak
truths" (56, *Selected* 116) and "fragments of the mother
lie open in all low places" (56, deleted in *Selected*). The

speaker, who has been "alone two days . . . walk[s] out
and return[s]" to "the body surround[ing him] on all
sides" and meets "a man from a milder planet" (56,
Selected 117).

> I say to him: "I know Christ is from your planet!"
> He lifts his eyes to me with a fierce light.
> He reaches out and touches me on the tip of my cock,
> and I fall asleep.
>
> I dream that the fathers are dying.
>
> (56, *Selected* 117)[26]

This gesture of the touch to the genital is ambiguous but, on the basis of what "happens" in the dream,
it seems to suggest the need to de-emphasize the masculine (let the fathers die) and assert the feminine
(gather together the fragments of the mother). As Jung
says, "The creative process has a feminine quality, and
the creative work arises from unconscious depths—we
might truly say from the realm of the Mothers."[27] In this
dream: "My shadow is underneath me, / floating in the
dark" and a "fireball floats" like "a light that comes
nearer when called! / A light the spirits turn their heads
for" (57).

The speaker recognizes that "The energy is inside
us. . . . / I start toward it, and meet an old man" (57,
Bly's ellipsis). This "old man" is the Jungian "wise old
man" who appears in dreams and visions as "an au-
thoritative voice." This "archetype . . . always appears
in a situation where insight, understanding, good ad-

vice, determination, planning, etc., are needed but cannot be mustered on one's own resources." And "the
intervention of the old man" is "indispensable, since
the conscious will by itself is hardly ever capable of
uniting the personality to the point where it acquires
this extraordinary power to succeed."[28] The speaker realizes that "much" is "beyond the reach of our eyes,"
things that "cannot be remembered and cannot be forgotten" (57, cf. "Some parts of me I cannot find now"
in *Selected*, [116]). And the "old man cries out: 'I am
here. / Either talk to me about your life, or turn
back' " (57).

The life told about is the three years alone in New
York, put into the context of the Jonah myth, of "three
days inside a warm-blooded fish" when " 'I saw the
road' " and " 'A whale bore me back home' " (58, *Selected* 117) to a symbolic rebirth. This rebirth initiates the
night journey of the next poem.[29]

"The Night Journey in the Cooking Pot" (59–63), the
longest poem in the sequence, is reduced in *Selected*
(118) to two stanzas (only one, the first, from the original poem) and is retitled "December 23, 1926," the date
of Bly's birth. "The Night Journey . . ." begins with an
interesting double criss-cross back to "Meeting the
Man Who Warns Me." The last line of "Meeting
the Man . . ." ends, "This joy I love is like wounds
at sea . . ." (58, Bly's ellipsis), and "The Night
Journey . . ." begins, "I was born during the night sea-
journey" (59). Further, the "three years alone" and the
"three days inside a warm-blooded fish" and the "I saw

the road . . . / A whale bore me back home" (58) at the end of "Meeting the Man . . ." is picked up again, both in terms of the imagery and the theme (an old theme, going back to Bly's beginnings) at the outset of "The Night Journey . . .":

> I float on solitude as on water . . . there is a road. . . .
> I felt the road first in New York, in that great room
> reading Rilke in the womanless loneliness.
> How marvelous the great wings sweeping along the floor,
> inwardness, inwardness, inwardness,
> the inward path I still walk on,
>
> (59, Bly's ellipses)

This metaphor of the road, particularly of an inward watery road, is as old as *Silence in the Snowy Fields* and it will become, before "Sleepers" ends, the key image of Bly's continuing quest in this book. (The "winter privacy" and the snow falling here in this poem immediately reminds one of *Silence* and of the "Six Winter Privacy Poems" which begin this book.) It ought perhaps also to be mentioned that the "night sea-journey" here about to be literally embarked on is clearly a pun on the visionary experience which is crucial to the whole poem; the sea-journey is also a *see*-journey. The fact that Bly has retitled this poem with the date of his birthday suggests a literal birth from physical waters, the amniotic fluid of his mother's womb, to the metaphysical waters of his dream-like, sea/see journey.

SLEEPERS JOINING HANDS

> Someone is asleep in the back of my house
> I feel the blood galloping in the body,
> the baby whirling in the womb.
> Dark bodies pass by far out at the horizon,
> trailing lights like flying saucers,
> the shadows go by long after the bodies have passed.
>   (60)

In the new stanza added in *Selected* Bly says, "I call out my wateriness in magnificent words" (*Selected*, 118).

"And so it happens that if anyone . . . undertakes for himself the perilous journey into the darkness by descending . . . into the crooked lanes of his own spiritual labyrinth, he soon finds himself in a landscape of symbolic figures. . . ."[30] The body of "The Night Journey . . ." is such a landscape of symbolic figures, but the basic movement and direction is never lost sight of: "For we are like the branch bent in the water . . . / Taken out, it is whole, it was always whole. . . ." (61, Bly's ellipses). This wholeness is a unity between the "underneath," the unconscious, and the conscious, between the awakened and the dreaming mind. And this unity *is* the road, sensed and understood ("I see the road ahead" [61], "I am on the road" [62]) even if never fully or satisfactorily realized ("What I have written is not good enough. / Who does it help?" 63). In this "night journey in the cooking pot" everything is mixed and merged, boiled in the brain during dream; everything is internalized.

In one of the most interesting passages in the poem, even the Biblical story of Jesus' birth and the events surrounding it is told as if it happened internally. "The King . . . . / sends his wise men out along the arteries . . . / to kill the child in the old moonlit villages of the brain" (62). This account is particularly interesting from a Jungian point of view because Jung identifies Christ as "our nearest analogy of the self and its meaning,"[31] and describes the self as "the archetype of unity and totality . . . the hypothetical point between conscious and unconscious . . . the God within."[32] Bly's attempts, here and elsewhere, to "domesticate the sublime" have been described by Charles Molesworth, who suggests that "the body becomes 'the field of consciousness' " within which the ecstatic may become divine, that, for Bly, the body becomes the "privileged term in the traditional body-soul dichotomy."[33] Still, there is a conflict with even this semi-divine body. When the speaker "think[s] I am the body, / the body rushes in and ties me up" (62) and at the end of the poem, "I sit down again, I hit my own body, / I shout at myself, I see what I have betrayed" (63).

At the end of "The Night Journey . . ." the sleeper is awake and ready to "join hands" with the "you" of the first line of "Water Drawn Up Into the Head" (64–67), the final poem of "Sleepers" and *Sleepers*. (Only four lines of "Water Drawn Up Into the Head" have been saved, revised and retitled "The Man Locked Inside the Oak" in *Selected* [125].)

"Water Drawn Up Into the Head" (64–67), as already suggested, completes the "book of my confessions" begun in its companion poem, "Water Under the Earth," at the beginning of the book, as Bly pulls the structure of the book tight toward its close. "Water Drawn Up Into the Head" begins:

> Now do you understand the men who laugh all
>   night in their sleep?
> Here is some prose:
>> *Once there was a man who went to a far*
>> *country to get his inheritance and then returned.*
>
> (64)

This prose passage describes precisely what the poem has done. The "far country" is the psyche and the "inheritance" has been the realization of inwardness—what the poem will describe as "the curved energy," or "another being living inside me" (65).

> So rather than saying that Christ is God or he is not,
> it is better to forget all that
> and lose yourself in the curved energy.
> I entered that energy one day,
> that is why I have lived alone in old places,
> that is why I have knelt in churches, weeping,
> that is why I have become a stranger to my father.
> We have no name for you, so we say:
> he makes grass grow upon the mountains,
> and gives food to the dark cattle of the sea,
> he feeds the young ravens that call on him.
>
> (65)

The religious quest that the whole poem has taken

is here described in terms of a variation on the parable of the prodigal son, another story of a return home after a time of wandering. The two brothers in the Biblical story, and the literal and psychological divisions throughout *Sleepers* between two brothers, make the allusion to the prodigal son story even more obvious. At the end of the story in the Bible the father tells the brother who has stayed home to rejoice in his brother's return, "For this thy brother was dead, and is alive again; and was lost, and is found" (Luke 15:32). Something very much like this symbolic salvation occurs here at the end of Bly's book.[34]

Of course, the prodigal son story is only one of many stories of journeying away from home and returning. Indeed, such stories are extremely common in fairy tales and Bly has been increasingly interested in fairy tales and the commentary on them, and especially interested in the work of Marie-Louise von Franz in books like *Problems of The Feminine in Fairytales* (1972), *Shadow and Evil in Fairytales* (1974), and *An Introduction to the Psychology of Fairy Tales* (1978). In many fairy tales and in psychic quests there is the inevitable "bringing back" to consciousness of something which has been lost or lost track of, submerged in the psyche, just as in this poem the water, symbolic of the unconscious (feminine) "mysterious mother" (66) has been "drawn up into the head," symbolic of the conscious (male) mind. Still, the Biblical story that Bly uses seems more pertinent to a reading of the poem than any of the more secular versions of the same essential story.

"Water Drawn Up Into the Head" is divided into two almost equal sections. The first section begins with a rhetorical question, directly addressed to "you." Clearly, this "you" is both a "we" ("we come face to face with you" 64) and an "I" merged, as the personal quest of the poem becomes universal, a "song of myself" which, like Walt Whitman's, becomes a song of all selves[35] and "That is why I am so glad . . . / I walk out, throw my arms up, and am glad" (65).

This gladness makes possible *"An Extra Joyful Chorus for Those Who Have Read This Far,"* conclusion to poem and book. The "chorus" is, literally, a private, meditative moment. ("I sit alone late at night. / I sit with eyes closed, thoughts shoot through me" 66.) But it is also almost a public declamation, rhetorically intoned, almost chanted (over half of the lines begin "I am"). The chorus is self-conscious with what it has uncovered in consciousness, what it has been able to express in poetry: "Sometimes when I read my own poems late at night, / I sense myself on a long road, / I feel the naked thing alone in the universe" (66).

This "naked thing alone in the universe" takes many forms:

> I have floated in the eternity of the cod heaven,
> I have felt the silver of infinite numbers brush my side—
> I am the crocodile unrolling and slashing through the
>   mudded water,
> I am the baboon crying out as her baby falls from the tree,
> I am the light that makes the flax blossom at midnight!

> I am an angel breaking into three parts over the Ural
>   Mountains!
> I am no one at all.
>
> (66–67)

This passage is interesting in several ways. It begins and ends with puns. "In the eternity of the cod heaven" catches up the various allusions to the Bible and fish that have run throughout the poem and the book; the assertion, "I am no one" suggests not only one, but a universal "one" made up of the many. This is the "angel breaking into three parts" which suggests the "three brains" in the trinity of "crocodile" (reptile brain), "baboon" (mammal brain), and "the light" (the new brain—"the mark of the new brain is light").[36]

Although this theory of the "three brains" is only alluded to here at the end of Bly's poem, it is important to his thinking because it provides the means of linking his earlier notion of "leaping poetry" to his reading of myth, archetype, and fairy tale.

Bly's basis for the "three brains" comes from the neurologist Paul MacLean, as applied by Arthur Koestler. MacLean says, "Man finds himself in the predicament that Nature has endowed him essentially with three brains which, despite great differences in structure, must function together and communicate with one another." He goes on, "The oldest of these brains is basically reptilian. The second has been inherited from lower mammals, and the third is a late mammalian development, which in its culmination in primates, has made man peculiarly man."[37] Koestler says that "maturation seems to mean a transition from the domination of the old brain towards the domination of the new" and that "poetry could thus be said to achieve a synthesis between the sophisticated reasoning of the neocortex and the more primitive emotional ways of the old brain," which he describes as a "draw-back-to-leap process." What this means is that "internal feelings are blended with what is seen, heard or otherwise sensed in such a way that the outside world is experienced as though it were inside."[38] "The creative act always involves a regression to earlier, more primitive levels in the mental hierarchy" and "the poetic image attains its highest vibrational intensity . . . when it strikes archetypal chords—when eternity looks through the window of time."[39]

There is one further stanza of "I am's" before the poem opens again, finally—at its close—to contain all the "sleepers in the world" whose "hands rush toward each other through miles of space" and "join" (67). "Our faces shine with the darkness" (67) here at the end of the poem. This oxymoron seems appropriate. *Sleepers Joining Hands* is, finally, a book not about "the light around the body" but a book about the light within.

Notes

1. Robert Bly, *Sleepers Joining Hands* (New York: Harper & Row, 1973) 3–4. Reprinted in *Selected* 56–57. Hereafter, references to *Sleepers* will be included in the text.

2. Bly, *Leaping Poetry* 1.

3. In terms of the revision of the *Sleepers* section in *Selected*, Bly has said, "The poems in *Selected Poems* from that section *amount* to new poems, although each of them is a kind of tree made by grafting a branch from the older tree. . . . I gave those lines that I loved new roots or new skin or new bark." (Letter to the author, Aug. 20, 1986.)

4. Joyce Carol Oates, "Where They All Are Sleeping," *Modern Poetry Studies* 4:3 (Winter, 1973): 341.

5. Bly, *Poetry Reading* 7. Bly wants, like Whitman in *Specimen Days*, to write the "interior history" of the war, "the real war" that will "never get in the books," "the untold and unwritten history of the war—infinitely greater (like life's) than the few scraps and distortions that are ever told or written." (*The Portable Walt Whitman* [New York: Viking, 1945] 587–588.)

6. Bly, "Whitman's Line as a Public Form," *Selected* 194–195, 197. It is perhaps not surprising to discover that Bly wrote "Teeth Mother" "somewhat with my voice," speaking "parts aloud at readings many times before I wrote them down" (*Talking* 201).

7. Many of the ideas and some of the lines in "Teeth Mother," among them these, appear in somewhat different form in Bly's only play, "The Satisfaction of Vietnam," *Chelsea*, 24/25 (Oct. 1968): 32–47.

8. David Cavitch, "Poet as Victim and Victimizer," *New York Times Book Review*, 18 Feb. 1973, 3.

9. Bly, *Talking* 251.

10. Nelson, *Robert Bly: An Introduction* 84–85.

11. It is interesting to compare Bly's "Mother Prayer" with this "restored" Old Testament passage. "Mother Prayer" reads:

Our Mother who are on earth
Your name was always holy
Your kingdom has already arrived
In the soul of the body
May we make each day our own bread
And may we forgive everyone
Even those who have not trespassed against us
Lead us not into disease

SLEEPERS JOINING HANDS

And save us from the longing we have to damage ourselves
For the body is yours, and energy and ecstasy
For ever and ever.

(See Shepherd Bliss, "Balancing Feminine & Masculine: The Mother Conference in Maine," *East West Journal* 8 [1978]: 39.)

12. Charles Molesworth, *The Fierce Embrace: A Study of Contemporary American Poetry* (Columbia: University of Missouri Press, 1979) 120.

13. Michael Atkinson, "*Sleepers Joining Hands:* Shadow and Self," *Iowa Review* 7:4 (Fall, 1976): 135, 145.

14. Nelson, *Robert Bly: An Introduction* 100.

15. Sugg, *Robert Bly* 87, 102. Other substantial readings of the poem are Ingegerd Friberg's in *Moving Inward: A Study of Robert Bly's Poetry* (Göteborg, Sweden, Acta Universitatis Gothoburgensis, 1977) 145–177; David Seal's "Waking to 'Sleepers Joining Hands' " and William V. Davis's " 'At the Edges of the Light': A Reading of Robert Bly's *Sleepers Joining Hands,*" both included in Jones and Daniels, *Solitude and Silence* 219–248; 250–267.

16. Denise Levertov, *The Poet in the World* (New York: New Directions, 1973) 3, 5.

17. See *Talking* 136, and Baker, *Solitude and Silence* 66.

18. Bly, *Talking* 136.

19. On a recent tape recording of his "Selected Poems" Bly says about "Sleepers": "The poem is a big mess. . . . So when I did my *Selected Poems* I pulled out sections and rewrote them and put them back into some more honest form." (Robert Bly, "Selected Poems," ed. William Booth [St. Paul, MN: Ally Press, 1987], vol. two.)

20. *The Essential Jung* (Princeton: Princeton University Press, 1983) 91.

21. *Essential Jung* 159, 221.

22. Bly, "Stevens and Jekyll," Heyen, *American Poets* 4.

23. *Essential Jung* 389.

24. Bly, "Stevens and Jekyll," Heyen, *American Poets* 4.

25. The revision of this section in *Selected* is entitled "A Dream of a Brother," which further emphasizes the theme, but may also be

important for Bly in a more personal way. Bly's only brother, James, was killed in an auto accident in 1971, and it seems clear, in several different contexts, that Bly merges his literal dead brother and a "dream-brother." (See Nelson, *Robert Bly: An Introduction* 240-241, n. 37.)

26. In the *Selected* version the touch on the cock puts the speaker to sleep: "He . . . touches me on the tip of the cock, / and I fall asleep. How beautiful that sleep is" (117).

27. C. G. Jung, *The Spirit in Man, Art, and Literature (Collected Works*, vol. 15) trans. R. F. C. Hull (Princeton: Princeton University Press, 1971) 103.

28. C. G. Jung, *Four Archetypes (Collected Works*, vol. 9, part 1) trans. R. F. C. Hull (Princeton: Princeton University Press, 1970) 93, 94, 98.

29. Arthur Koestler associates the "night journey" with the story of Jonah and the whale and describes it as a transition in which "consciousness becomes unborn—to become reborn." (*The Act of Creation* [New York: Macmillan, 1964] 360.) Cf. "The idea that the passage of the magical threshold is a transit into a sphere of rebirth is symbolized in the worldwide womb image of the belly of the whale." (Joseph Campbell, *The Hero with a Thousand Faces* [Princeton: Princeton University Press, 1968] 90.)

30. Campbell, *Hero with a Thousand Faces* 101.

31. *Essential Jung* 299. Cf. 229, 332.

32. *Essential Jung* 19-20. Cf. 242, 267.

33. Molesworth, *Fierce Embrace* 136-137.

34. It is perhaps inevitable, in this context, to remember Bly's complex relationship to his only brother, James, who stayed at home on the family farm while Robert "wandered."

35. For more on the correspondences between Bly's poem and Whitman (both "Song of Myself" and "The Sleepers") see William V. Davis's " 'At the Edges of the Light,' " in Jones and Daniels, *Of Solitude and Silence* 260, 266-267.

36. Bly, *Leaping Poetry* 62. For Bly's thinking on the "three brains" see *Leaping Poetry* 59-67 and *Talking* 41-44; for a consideration of Bly's sources on this theory in Koestler, Paul MacLean and others see Wil-

liam V. Davis's " 'At the Edges of the Light,' " in Jones and Daniels, *Of Solitude and Silence* 257–259, 264–265.

37. Paul MacLean, "New Findings Relevant to the Evolution of Psychosexual Functions of the Brain," *Journal of Nervous and Mental Disease*, 135:4 (Oct. 1962): 289.

38. Arthur Koestler, *The Ghost in the Machine* (New York: Macmillan, 1968) 286, 288–289.

39. Koestler, *Act of Creation* 316, 353.

CHAPTER FIVE

The Morning Glory and *This Body is Made of Camphor and Gopherwood*

Bly has suggested that prose poems begin to appear when the culture of a period gets dangerously close to abstractions, when its "poetry gets too abstract."[1] It is almost as if the prose poem surfaces in specific situations as a way of maintaining poetry in an age about to abandon it. This notion is interesting in its own right, but it is all the more interesting in that, following *Sleepers*, a book which tended to veer toward abstraction, Bly turned, in *The Morning Glory* and *This Body is Made of Camphor and Gopherwood*,[2] to the prose poem which, he said, "helps to balance that abstraction,"[3] or "helps to heal the wound of abstraction."[4]

Because Bly tends to see himself as paradigm of the poet, it is perhaps not surprising that he should attempt to define the age through defining himself. He may well be right that American culture, in the mid-1970s, was going through a major period of reform, and moving increasingly toward abstraction. Following *Sleepers*, Bly himself was going through a period of renewal. That renewal is evident both in the new form of the prose poem that he turned to in this period and in the images and themes of *Morning Glory* and *This Body*, which return so insistently to the world of *Silence in the Snowy Fields* and the "Six Winter Privacy Poems" of *Sleepers*. It is almost as if Bly returned so conspicuously (perhaps even unconsciously) to his own poetic beginnings because he knew, or sensed, that he had moved dangerously close to abstraction himself, and also because he realized that he was on the verge of a new beginning.

The last chapter suggested that *Sleepers* was a book not about the light around the body but about the light within the body. Echoing this notion in his recent *Selected Poems* Bly says that in the prose poems, "it was as if I had descended into the body."[5] But there is a paradox here too, as Bly notes in his epigraph to *Morning Glory*: "There is an old occult saying: whoever wants to see the invisible has to penetrate more deeply into the visible."[6] This use of the visible to penetrate the invisible is, of course, a central thesis in much of Bly's work but it is particularly evident in his prose poems. Indeed, the history and practice of the prose poem almost demands such a tactic, a fact which Bly acknowledges by associating these poems with the " 'seeing' poems of Rilke, and the 'object' poems of Francis Ponge."[7] "One sort of prose poem comes from the long tradition of the fable; another from the tradition of colorful and spectacular writing, as in Rimbaud's *Illuminations*; the prose poems I write belong to the tradition of Jiménez and Francis Ponge, and pays [*sic*] respect to their love of minute particulars."[8] Something paradoxical and unique occurs in these poems, particularly the poems of *This Body*, those "hushed pointers to the ineffable,"[9] where "vision in emptiness often becomes . . . vision of the invisible."[10]

Russell Edson, one of the most prolific practitioners of the prose poem, has suggested an important distinction between poetry and prose. Edson says, "Time flows *through* prose, and *around* poetry. Poetry is the sense of the permanent, of time held. Prose is the sense of *normal* time, time flowing. . . . And it is the two edges of contradictory time touching, fusing in unlikely combinations that creates the central metaphor of the prose poem."[11] Although this is not the place to try to define the form of the prose poem or to describe its history,[12] it might be noted that Michael Benedikt has written a very helpful introduction to the prose poem in his anthology on the genre. He details five "special properties" of the form: "attention to the unconscious and its particular logic," "an accelerated use of colloquial and other everyday speech patterns," "a visionary thrust," humor and/or irony, and "hopeful skepticism." Benedikt sees in Bly's discussion of the "image-oriented poetry of the 1960s" and the "technique of informality" in his essay "Looking for Dragon Smoke" (which Benedikt calls "a critical piece which bids fair to become as central to our time as 'Tradition and the Individual Talent' was to Eliot's") the "break-through toward the prose poem" in this country.[13]

Bly, in a short but important comment on the prose poem, says, "In a prose poem we often feel a man or woman talking not before a crowd but in a low voice to

THE MORNING GLORY AND THIS BODY IS MADE OF CAMPHOR AND GOPHERWOOD

someone he is sure is listening."[14] Bly's prose poems in *Morning Glory* and *This Body* are poems spoken "in a low voice to someone he is sure is listening."

Like both *Silence in the Snowy Fields* and *This Tree Will Be Here for a Thousand Years*, books to which this book returns in theme and design, *The Morning Glory* contains forty-four poems. Of these, fourteen are newly collected in this edition; the others are reprinted, some revised and/or retitled, from two earlier editions of *The Morning Glory* (twelve poems in 1969, twenty in 1970) and from *Point Reyes Poems*, a limited edition of ten poems published in 1974.

The first poem in *Morning Glory*, "A Bird's Nest Made of White Reed Fiber" (3) sets both the tone and the apocalyptic theme of the whole volume:

> The nest is white as the foam thrown up when the sea hits rocks! It is translucent as those cloudy transoms above Victorian doors, and swirled as the hair of those intense nurses, gray and tangled after long nights in Crimean wards. It is something made and then forgotten, like our own lives that we will entirely forget in the grave, when we are floating, nearing the shore where we will be reborn, ecstatic and black.

The prose poems of *Morning Glory*, like this bird's nest, are "something made and then forgotten," but, at the same time they stand, symbolically, for the eternal in man since they exist near "the shore where we will be reborn, ecstatic and black." Ecstasy is a key (and an overused) word in Bly's prose poems and the "black" at the end of this poem suggests the dark apocalypse so many of the poems explore. In his essay on the prose poem Bly indirectly alludes to this poem when he says: "It's possible that while a bird is building its nest an idea for a song it has never sung rises to its small head. So there are certain thoughts and impulses to thoughts in us that flow upward and into the head only when the psyche is calm, and only while language is being used. Buried impulses toward joy are carried upward on the artesian well of the prose poem."[15] This metaphor of the prose poem tapping the internal pressure of deep waters within the psyche and allowing them to flow up toward the surface obviously suggests the "deep images" and the Boehmean landscape of *Silence* as well as the Jungian depths of poems like "Water Under the Earth" and "Water Drawn Up Into the Head" of *Sleepers.*

"A Hollow Tree" (11, *Selected* 91) typifies the tactic of many of the prose poems in *Morning Glory.* It begins with the very realistic, even mundane, experience of being out walking, seeing a hollow stump and looking into it. But, as Ralph Mills says, "The feeling of factual accuracy lasts . . . just [long] enough to provide a context for what follows and to lead the reader to the place where vision takes command."[16] Inside the stump are "Siamese temple walls . . . all brown and ancient," which "have been worked on by the intricate ones." These Siamese temple walls suggest the fusion of inner and outer, the physical and the metaphysical, the "pri-

THE MORNING GLORY AND THIS BODY IS MADE OF CAMPHOR AND GOPHERWOOD

vacy and secrecy" which so many of these prose poems explore. The "gray feathers" scattered on "the temple floor" at the end of the poem, with their hint of sacrifice or sacred ceremony, haunt the imagination and memory back beyond the time where man can go. As Bly says in his essay, "The Prose Poem as an Evolving Form," "When the human mind honors a stump, for example, by giving it human attention in the right way, something in the soul is released; and often through the stump we receive information we wouldn't have received by thinking or by fantasy" (*Selected* 201-202).

The most ambitious and the longest poem in *Morning Glory* is "The Hockey Poem" (14-17, revised in *Selected* 100-102), dedicated to Bly's old friend and collaborator, William Duffy.[17] It is an important poem both for what it attempts and because it largely fails. (In the *Selected* version, in addition to internal revision, Bly has divided the poem into four numbered and titled sections, the first and last headed "The Goalie," the two middle sections entitled "The Attack" and "Trouble." The significance of the poem for Bly, and the difficulty he has had with it, seem obvious. Clearly, too, he wishes to save it for its significance to his canon.)

"The Hockey Poem" begins by comparing the Boston College hockey team to Roman centurions, but the focus quickly turns to the "goalie." Immediately, the conspicuous self-consciousness of the poem becomes clear in terms of the formal name for a goalie—a goalkeeper. If is as if Bly is simultaneously setting out the goals of his poetry and attempting to keep to them during the game of the poem. The poem contains many of the most overt themes in Bly's work. The goalie "guarding a basket with nothing in it" (14), "looks prehistoric with his rhinoceros legs . . . as if he's going to become extinct" (14); he "is the old witch in the woods, waiting for the children to come home" (14), "a mother hen" (15), "like a white insect, who has given up on evolution in this life" (16), "as ominous as a Middle Ages ["Dark Ages" in *Selected*] knight" (16–17), "the old woman in the shoe" (17) and finally "not a man at all, but a woman, all women," "a woman weeping over the children of men" into whose "cage everything disappears in the end" (17). "And at the end, she is still waiting, brushing away the leaves, waiting for the new children developed by speed, by war . . ." (17, Bly's ellipsis). There are other equally conflicting images in the poem. Clearly, Bly is fascinated by this game played over frozen water with a fast-moving puck in which points are scored by hitting the puck into a net, a goal. The game precisely duplicates Bly's method in many of his most representative, and most accomplished and successful, poems. If "The Hockey Poem" does not fully succeed as a poem, it succeeds in describing Bly's methodology in graphic terms. And it carries its own built-in congratulation: "how beautiful, like the body and soul crossing in a poem" (16). This "crossing" is precisely what Bly always aims for, and often succeeds in accomplishing.

The very excesses which flaw "The Hockey Poem" make for some of Bly's most effective poems when he more tightly controls his metaphors and the structure of the poem. Length itself may have something to do with the problems in "The Hockey Poem." As Edson says, "The properly made prose poem is *short* . . . thus, whatever story-telling is necessary . . . must depend on images rather than on bridges of description."[18] Bly has seldom been interested in or successful with long narrative poems; his temperament seems to be more attuned to the lyric, and, even in the prose poem, when he stays closest to the lyric he is most successful.

"The Point Reyes Poems," the ten-poem sequence that makes up the central section of *Morning Glory,* is an especially strong group of poems. The sequence opens with "November Day at McClure's" and the penultimate poem in the sequence is "The Dead Seal near McClure's Beach." These two poems frame the sequence and provide the central focus for it and for the whole book.

In "November Day at McClure's" (39, *Selected* 90) the poet is alone on the lonely beach as the sea and the sky grow "more and more private." Things are at their edges, on the verge of disappearing: "The unobserved water rushes out to the horizon, horses galloping in a mountain valley at night." High "on the worn top" of rock, "forty feet up," there are stranded "flags of seaweed" and "separated water still pooled." This barren seascape reminds the poet of "black ducks that fly desolate, forlorn, and joyful over the seething swells." This is an interesting trinity: "desolate" and "forlorn" are almost synonyms and are used with an antonym—

"joyful". The natural creatures in this natural place "never 'feel pity for themselves,' and 'do not lie awake weeping for their sins,' "[19] but go about their business at peace with the transitory world they inhabit: "The vultures coast with furry necks extended, watching over the desert for signs of life to end." They know what needs to be learned: "Inside us there is some secret. We are following a narrow ledge around a mountain, we are sailing on skeletal eerie craft over the buoyant ocean" (39).

"The Dead Seal near McClure's Beach" (52–54, revised and retitled "The Dead Seal" in *Selected* 96–97) seems to take up where "November Day at McClure's" left off. Moving from "the jagged rock at the south end of McClure's Beach" (39) in "November Day" and "Walking north toward the point" the poet comes "on a dead seal":

> From a few feet away, he looks like a brown log. The body is on its back, dead only a few hours. I stand and look at him. There's a quiver in the dead flesh: My God, he's still alive. And a shock goes through me, as if a wall of my room had fallen away.
>
> (*Selected* 96)

When he realizes that the seal is not dead, but dying, he wonders what to do. He knows that the reason the seal is dying is that it has gotten into oil ("that heats our houses so efficiently"). He knows there is, really, nothing he can do and he knows, most importantly, that the seal doesn't want anything to be done; he wants only to be left alone with his dying, his death.

    I reach out and touch him. Suddenly he rears up, turns over. He gives three cries: Awaark! Awaark! Awaark!—like the cries from Christmas toys. He lunges toward me; I am terrified and leap back, though I know there can be no teeth in that jaw. He starts flopping toward the sea. But he falls over, on his face. He does not *want* to go back to the sea. He looks up at the sky, and he looks like an old lady who has lost her hair. He puts his chin back down on the sand, rearranges his flippers, and waits for me to go. I go. The next day I go back to say goodbye. He's dead now. But he's not. He's a quarter mile farther up the shore. Today he is thinner, squatting on his stomach, head out. The ribs show more: each vertebra on the back under the coat is visible, shiny. He breathes in and out.

    A wave comes in, touches his nose. He turns and looks at me—the eyes slanted; the crown of his head looks like a boy's leather jacket bending over some bicycle bars. He is taking a long time to die. The whiskers white as porcupine quills, the forehead slopes. . . . Goodbye, brother; die in the sound of waves. Forgive us if we have killed you. Long live your race, your inner-tube race, so uncomfortable on land, so comfortable in the ocean. Be comfortable in death then, when the sand will be out of your nostrils, and you can swim in long loops through

the pure death, ducking under as assassinations
break above you. You don't want to be touched by
me. I climb the cliff and go home the other way.
(*Selected*, 96–97, Bly's ellipsis)

This encounter with the dying seal is only one of
many in which Bly describes some sort of confrontation
with an animal. In these prose poems in particular animals seem to be especially conspicuous. Bly has said,
"The difference between lulling prose and the good
prose poem is that the urgent, alert rhythm of the prose
poem prepares us to journey, to cross the border, either
to the other world, or to that place where the animal
lives" (*Selected*, 88). Or, again, "What is precious in
poetry is the inwardness and the love of animals"
(*Talking*, 32).

The animals are always fully realized, as real as this
dying seal, and at the same time they seem symbolic of
a condition or situation which, if man does not now
fully participate in, he seems to be able to sympathize
with. It seems almost to be a condition or a relationship
that man and the animals share in equally and can communicate across, a condition or a relationship or an at-
tribute that man has almost forgotten and that the
animal can teach him again. The dignity in the face of
death that the dying seal exhibits in this poem is worthy
of the best human behavior and a man can learn a les-
son from such reserve and such an example. The fact
that the seal is an amphibian, equally at home on water
and land, is particularly apt in a poem that attempts to

cross over borders, to serve as intermediary between man and the animal kingdom.

Along these lines, and in terms of many of the poems of *Morning Glory*, Bly, who has translated Rilke, seems to be thinking of his *Elegies:*

> With all its eyes the natural world looks out into the Open. Only *our* eyes are turned backward, and surround plant, animal, child like traps, as they emerge into their freedom. We know what is really out there only from the animal's gaze.
>
>   * * *
>
> If the animal moving toward us so securely in a different direction had our kind of consciousness—, it would wrench us around and drag us along its path.
>
>   * * *
>
> And we: spectators, always, everywhere, . . .[20]

In "Sunday Morning in Tomales Bay" (45–46) there are more seals, in this case the large Pacific eared seals known as sea lions, and a great blue heron. The scene is simple, the action slight, and yet there is the sense of something special about this Sunday morning meditation. The "we" in the boat are suddenly drifting, lost. Through the fog "we" think "we" see an oil derrick, but discover "it is alive! It is a Great Blue Heron!" who, "walks away . . . like some old Hittite empire" (45, Bly's ellipsis) purged of "all the brutality . . . only the rare vases left, and the elegant necks of the women." Where the heron was there is now a sea of sea lions,

who, like the Hittite heron and the Sunday morning
meditation, remind us of Biblical texts, of something
somehow holy, that has come from another world to
look into ours: "The whiskered heads peer over at us
attentively, like angels called to look at a baby. They
have risen from their sea-mangers to peer at us. Their
Magi come to them every day . . . and they gaze at the
godless in their wooden boat"(45).[21] This epiphanic moment is brief, but it is important. It prepares the reader
for the more detailed and explicit Christian symbolism
which is to come at the end of this section of the book
and in the final section of the book.

When the boat drifts near the "fogged" shore, boulders suddenly materialize as more sea lions, "hundreds
of them!," which abruptly start "to roll seaward" as
"the heron slowly ascends" and then "flies away thin as
a grassblade in the fog" (45).

The final section of *Morning Glory* brings the book
to a strong conclusion. "August Rain" is typical of
many of the best poems in *Morning Glory* but, perhaps
more importantly, it brings the poet back to the human
community again after so much time spent alone, and it
looks forward to the poems to come in *The Man in the
Black Coat Turns* and *Loving a Woman in Two Worlds*.

"August Rain," (69–70, *Selected* 103–104) set in the
late summer, turns the book toward the end of the year.
In one sense the whole of *Morning Glory* suggests such
a turning, since it celebrates a period of transition in the
poet's life in terms of a cycle of transition in nature. As

we shall see, the book will end with the turning of the year, the beginning of another new year.

Speaking of the genesis of "August Rain," Bly says: "One August day watching a rain shower, I was astounded at how many separate events were taking place, each taking place only once. Each needed to be given space in the poem separately, and I was glad for the prose poem form."[22]

There is a kind of calm in "August Rain," an overcoming of "the category [of] mind that makes mutually exclusive inner and outer, human and animal, reason and instinct."[23] The poem begins with "a cheerful thunder" and the poet "buoyant and affectionate" going "indoors to find my children." He "feel[s] triumphant" in the knowledge that "what has failed and been forgiven" is part of the natural, inevitable, movement toward "feel[ing] a part of the dead straw of the universe" like the "objects that belong to us," which, ultimately, we will become part of. Looking forward toward the end, there is the feeling of peace, rest. The mood and tone of this poem, and of many of the poems in this section, is perhaps best captured in the lovely poem, "Grass from Two Years" (71–72, *Selected* 109):

> When I write poems, I need to be near grass
> that no one else sees, as in this spot, where I sit for
> an hour under the cottonwood. The long grass has
> fallen over until it flows. Whatever I am . . . if the
> great hawks come to look for me, I will be here in

this grass. Knobby twigs have dropped on it. The summer's grass still green crosses some dry grass beneath, like the hair of the very old, that we stroke in the morning.

And how beautiful this ring of dry grass is, pale and tan, that curves around the half-buried branch—the grass flows over it, and is pale, gone, ascended, no longer selfish, no longer centered on its mouth; it is centered now on the God "of distance and of absence." Its pale blades lie near each other, circling the dry stick. It is a stick that the rain did not care for, and has ignored, as it fell in the night on men holding horses in the courtyard; and the sunlight was glad that the branch could be ignored, and did not ask to be loved—so I have loved you—and the branch and the grass lie here deserted, a part of the wild things of the world, noticed only for a moment by a heavy, nervous man who sits near them, and feels he has at this moment more joy that anyone alive (*Selected* 109).

The Morning Glory ends with two poems which deal with death and birth on the personal, the religious and the natural levels. Bly says that "prose poems . . . resemble home or private religion" and this kind of private religion, in "the ancient world," was called the "Mysteries."[24] In each of these poems there is a mystery, one religious and one natural, but both become personal.

"Christmas Eve Service at Midnight at St. Michael's" (73–74, *Selected* 105) brings to climax the Christian symbolism that has appeared earlier in the book and it brings together, too, the birth-death-rebirth trichotomy that is simultaneously celebrated in the Christmas Eve service, the year's turning, and by the poet's family who attend this Christmas service six months after James, Bly's only brother, has been killed in an automobile accident.

The poem begins, on this "cold night" with "the dark surround[ing] the frail wood houses, that were so recently trees," and the family leaving "my father's house an hour before midnight," for church. "Outside the snow labors its old Manichean labors" (73) and at midnight the service begins. The priest breaks the wafer, "a clear and terrifying sound . . . frightening . . . for like so many acts, it is permanent." Then the priest "tells us that Christ intended to leave his body behind . . . it is confusing . . . we take our bodies with us when we go" (74, Bly's ellipses). The mystery of the birth being celebrated in this service and inseparably linked to the ceremonies celebrating the death on Good Friday and the resurrection on Easter Sunday, both of which are symbolized here by the communion, is confusing in the context of the death of the poet's brother, who took his body with him when he died. At the end of the poem the poet experiences a dream or reverie in which he sees "oceans dark and lifting near flights of stairs, oceans lifting and torn . . . stirred and calmed" over which "a large man is flying . . . with wings spread, a wound on his chest" (74).

This conclusion is reminiscent of a passage on "reverie and cosmos" in Bachelard's *Poetics of Reverie:*

> When a dreamer of reveries has swept aside all the
> "preoccupations" which were encumbering his
> everyday life, when he has detached himself from
> the worry which comes to him from the worry of
> others, when he is thus truly the *author of his
> solitude,* when he can finally contemplate a beautiful
> aspect of the universe without counting the minutes,
> that dreamer feels a being opening within him.
> Suddenly such a dreamer is a *world dreamer.* He
> opens himself to the world, and the world opens
> itself to him. . . . In a reverie of solitude which
> increases the solitude of the dreamer, two depths
> pair off, reverberate in echoes which go from the
> depths of being of the world to a depth of being of
> the dreamer. Time is suspended. Time no longer has
> any yesterday and no longer any tomorrow. Time is
> engulfed in the double depth of the dreamer and
> the world. The World is so majestic that nothing any
> longer happens there; the World reposes in its
> tranquility. The dreamer is tranquil before a tranquil
> Water.[25]

It is in the kind of reverie that the "Christmas Eve
Service" ends that "Opening the Door of a Barn I
Thought Was Empty on New Year's Eve" (75–76, *Selected*
106) begins. Even though the scene is literal enough, it
partakes of a mystical, dream-like quality. This is not
the usual fun-filled, crowd-oriented evening so typical

THE MORNING GLORY AND *THIS BODY IS MADE OF CAMPHOR AND GOPHERWOOD*

of New Year's Eve, but it seems, nonetheless, almost ritualistically planned for, a place sought out for the sake of the incipient mystery: "I got there by dusk. The west shot up a red beam. I open the double doors and go in. Sounds of breathing! Thirty steers are wandering around, the partitions gone. Creatures heavy, shaggy, slowly moving in the dying light. Bodies with no St. Teresas look straight at me" (75).

The poem ends:

These breathing ones do not demand eternal life, they ask only to eat the crushed corn, and the hay, coarse as rivers, and cross the rivers, and sometimes feel an affection run along the heavy nerves. They have the wonder and bewilderment of the whale, with too much flesh, the body with the lamp lit inside, fluttering on a windy night.

The body "with the lamp lit inside" here at the end of *Morning Glory* is the body that will be illuminated from within in the companion book of prose poems, *This Body Is Made of Camphor and Gopherwood*.

* * *

This Body Is Made of Camphor and Gopherwood (1977), a sequence of twenty prose poems, is a sequel to *The Morning Glory* formally and thematically. In it Bly continues to explore the genre of the prose poem and he extends his basically "religious" theme from *Morning Glory* into the realm of the ecstatic. As Charles Molesworth quite rightly says, *This Body* signals "a decisive change" in Bly's poetry. In it he "concentrates his vision more directly on ecstatic moments and writes what must be described as religious poetry," even though these "religious meditations" are written "for a public that is no longer ostensibly religious."[26]

In many ways, *This Body* continues the return to beginnings, the new beginning that *Morning Glory* initiated. In *Morning Glory*, but especially in *This Body*, Bly returns to the voice, the themes, even the sources of *Silence in the Snowy Fields*. Just as the major metaphor of *Silence* was sleep and awakening, it is the major metaphor in *This Body*. Just as Boehme and Jung were the major background sources for and influences on the early lined lyrics, their voices (more subtly interfused with the increasingly personal voice of Bly's speaker) are the major voices here.

This Body is divided into two equal parts. The first ten poems, often through dreams or visions, detail the "dream of what is missing" ("A Dream of What Is Missing" 27), while the second half of the book, the final ten poems, suggests the upswing of emotion, the heightened vision and perception typical of an ecstatic vision, a kind of "extra joyful chorus for those who have read this far." The two central poems in the book, "Walking to the Next Farm" (31–32) and "The Origin of the Praise of God" (35–36) work the transition between the two parts of the book. In terms of the metaphor that began the book ("Walking Swiftly" 13) here at the center of it poet and reader "walk" (a variation on the old "road" metaphor so important in the early books) to the "next

farm," into the "origin of the praise of God," the impetus for and the presence of the ecstatic moment with
which *This Body* concludes. Thus, the structural and
thematic pattern made so explicit in this book is basic to
Bly's structural and thematic design in many of his
books.

But *This Body* is unique in another way that needs to
be noticed. Each of these twenty prose poems is accompanied by a drawing of a snail shell by Gendron Jensen,
who is described in the cover blurb as "a forest eccen-
tric." This snail series was created specifically for Bly's
book by Jensen and the drawings work intricately with
the poems. The drawings are placed in sequence so that
when the pages of the book are riffled the snail shell
rises and simultaneously turns. In the first drawing the
shell lies with its opening turned away from the viewer,
but gradually it "opens" and, from the mid-point of the
book to the end, the open end remains in full view even
as the turning continues. The shell seems to rise up,
turn toward the reader and lie down again. "Closed" at
the beginning, it is "open" at the end, as if it has of its
own volition turned and opened itself. Thus the snail
shell becomes a visual emblem of the theme the poems
themselves suggest, or even demand from the reader—a
turning and ultimately an opening to them.[27]

"Walking Swiftly" (13, revised in *Selected* 131), the
first poem in the book, announces the dominant metaphor of the book, that of sleep and the awakening from
sleep, and suggests an immediate association between
these poems and many of Bly's earlier poems. It begins,

"When I wake," which, even though it suggests an awakening, has the "characteristics of a dream-vision."[28] This waking is both literal and metaphoric, an awakening to what D. H. Lawrence called "the audible unconscious."[29] Bly, of course, has been made very much aware of the "sleeping" side of the psyche and of the necessity of "awakening" to it through Boehme and Jung. For Jung, the dream "is specifically the utterance of the unconscious" that "operates in and out of waking existence."[30] And the relationship between the body, Bly's "this body," and consciousness itself is specific and definitive. As Jung puts it, "psyche and body are not separate entities but one and the same life."[31]

Thus, soon after "I wake, . . . All seems calm, and yet somewhere inside I am not calm." The reason for this is that "the heat inside the human body grows" and "does not know where to throw itself."[32] Part of the problem is that both inner and outer worlds are out of tune with the universe: "We live in modern buildings made of two-by-fours, [i.e., "square houses" in *Sleepers*, 33] making the landscape nervous for a hundred miles," as opposed to the Indians who do everything in circles "because the Power of the World always works in circles, and everything tries to be round" as Bly, quoting Black Elk, in *Sleepers* (33) says. And our "Emperor" "in his stone walls" (*Selected* 131), at sixty, calls "for rhinoceros horn, for sky-blue phoenix eggs," empty symbols of virility and regeneration, while around him the creatures of the world continue the rounds of their existences: "the wasps kept guard, the hens continued

their patrol, the oysters open and close all questions."
The poem ends with the poet, as artist, awakened to his
heat energy, his creative fire, and, conscious of its ultimate sources, going "swiftly to his studio" to carve
"oceanic waves into the dragon's mane" (13).[33] In terms
of Bly's dominant metaphor of light in his "three brain"
theory and in terms of the Jungian and Boehmean references scattered throughout his work, the poet-speaker-
artist has here *become* the light inside the body.

"The Left Hand" (15), the second poem in the
book, is one of two title poems (the other is "The Pail"
47). "My friend, this body is made of camphor and gopherwood. Where it goes, we follow even into the Ark."
Gopherwood was the material used to build the ark in
Genesis 6:14. As such, the gopherwood here, and the
camphor, are the visible symbols of the metaphysical
reality housed in the symbolic ark of the covenant. They
become the basic materials of "this body," this new en-
tity being born ("the body comes out hesitatingly"),
which is both physical and metaphysical.

"The Sleeper" (17) is explicitly a dream poem. The
sleeping dreamer, "all withdrawn into himself," is visited by two men, one who sits with him and one who
plays music for him, but neither can awaken him.[34] He
dreams of other "men suddenly appearing whom I did
not know, but who knew me." The unrecognized men
in this dream poem are, no doubt, visions of the father[s] found in the next poem, "Finding the Father"
(19), a poem that looks forward to more recent work,
especially to *The Man in the Black Coat Turns.* The way to

the father is through "this body." "This body offers to carry us for nothing. . . . We will go there, the body says, and there find the father whom we have never met, who . . . has lived . . . longing for his child, whom he saw only once," who is "lonely in his whole body, waiting for you" (19). And once the father has been found by the body, then the poet looks "from inside my body" (21), and discovers how we are divided between an earth-bound and a heavenward "body," described in terms of the heavenly bodies of the sun and moon, as the next poem, "Looking from Inside My Body" (21, revised and retitled "The Upward Moon and the Downward Moon" in *Selected* 133)[35] indicates.

The newly-born body "is a brilliant being, locked in the prison of human dullness" ("Going Out to Check the Ewes," 23). It is like a "watcher" within: "Inside us there is a listener who listens for what we say, a watcher who watches what we do . . . calling us into what is possible" ("The Watcher," *Selected* 135, the revision of "Falling into Holes in Our Sentences," *This Body* 29).

The first half of *This Body* ends with "Walking to the Next Farm" (31–32), a poem in which the transition the body has been going through is finally fully accomplished. The poem is set in a snowscape, by now the only appropriate landscape for epiphany in Bly. Moving "through the . . . powerful snow energy" the poet feels "as if a new body were rising, with tremendous swirls" within him. The "energy" is like the "background of flames" that arise from a "fierce man's hair." And what does all this mean? What is being "asked of us?" The answer combines most of what Bly has been building to all along, an integration of personality and psyche in terms of the Boehmean-Jungian prescription: "Then what is asked of us? To stop sacrificing one energy for another. They are not different energies anyway, not 'male' or 'female,' but whirls of different speeds as they revolve. We must learn to worship both." The poem ends with three lines in which the poet, now speaking in poetry per se envisions the "light" of the new energy and vitality in the new body:

> The light settles down in front of each snowflake,
> and the dark rises up behind it,
> and inside its own center it lives!

The second half of *This Body* begins with an extremely important poem, "The Origin of the Praise of God," (35–36, revised in *Selected* 136). It is dedicated to Lewis Thomas and his book, *The Lives of a Cell* (1974), a book that in some ways tries to reduce the whole of the earth to a single cell, just as Bly tries to describe the whole of the world in a single poem.[36]

"The Origin . . ." begins, "My friend, this body is made of bone and excited protozoa . . . and it is with my body that I love the fields. How do I know what I feel but what the body tells me?" (35, Bly's ellipsis). We walk through "the magnetic fields of other bodies" and "are drawn down into the sweetest pools of slowly circling energies." Then, as "the space between two people diminishes . . . they merge at last" and "clouds of cells far inside the body" awaken "and beings unknown to us start out in a pilgrimage to their Saviour, to their holy place." This holy place is "a small black stone, that they remember from Protozoic times, when it was rolled away from a door." And "the cells dance inside beams of sunlight so thin we cannot see them" and from "the dance of the cells praise sentences rise to the throat of the man praying and singing alone in his room" who "lets his arms climb above his head, and says, 'Now do you still say you cannot choose the Road?' " (35–36).

Obviously, this poem is packed with much of what Bly has been over in the past and with much of what he has been, and is, building to in this book. This "visionary hymn to the body . . . dramatizes an experience of the inner deity" and "is sanctioned at the close by the figure of a sage whose final question clarifies for the reader the route Bly's visionary pursuit in this prose poem sequence has traced."[37] There are, however, several details new, or newly envisioned in the poem. "This body" is described in terms of bone and protozoa (a word that is repeated four times after the first sentence), a reference to those single-celled creatures whose complex life-cycles and fitful movements duplicate the "leaping" imagery and rhythm of many of these poems. In only one of two lined tercets, or triplets, in the book (see "Walking to the Next Farm" above for the other)[38] Bly says:

> The sunlight lays itself down before the protozoa,
> the night opens itself out behind it,
> and inside its own energy it lives! (35)

THE MORNING GLORY AND THIS BODY IS MADE OF CAMPHOR AND GOPHERWOOD

Here the symbolism of illumination, the light-dark dichotomy, the "energy" of the psyche and the notion of the complicity and exchanges between body and spirit so frequently used by Bly are reduced to their most minute levels. The "holy Place" which "is a small black stone" surrealistically combines the Biblical reference to a new beginning and to life from death with the cellular one, as the poem both visions and envisions "the origins of the praise of God" in the actions of the universe described and detailed within the cells of a single body—or even the body of a single cell.

At this point most of what Bly wants to say in this book has been said, and he spends much of the remainder of the book recapitulating the themes and duplicating the metaphors already mentioned.

One poem in particular, the second title poem, "The Pail" (47), is especially important because it describes the mystical state (which Bly invariably depicts in terms of ecstatic experiences) that so many of the poems in *This Body* border on or attempt to realize. Internal rhyme and seasonal change ("the faint rain of March") and the Boehmean dichotomy of inner and outer ("the granary door turns dark on the outside, the oats inside still dry") emphasize the shifts of things which the poem documents.

Louis Martz's analysis of meditative verse is helpful here. According to Martz, the meditative poem "is a work that creates an interior drama . . . usually . . . by some form of self-address, and concludes with a moment of illumination, where the speaker's self has, for a time, found an answer to its conflicts."[39] Martz continues elsewhere, "This meditative kind of poetry consists of 'current language heightened' (Hopkins' phrase)—heightened by a voice that is at once that of a unique individual and yet still the voice of a man searching inwardly in common ways for the common bond of mankind."[40]

Thus, in the poems in the last half of *This Body* Bly describes: "love flow[ing] out and around in circles" ("Coming In for Supper" 39); a "body of water near where we sleep," where "all the images rearrange themselves" ("How the Ant Takes Part" 43); the "gathered ecstasies from my own body" ("The Pail" 47); "the body laboring before dawn to understand its dream" ("Snow Falling on Snow"[49], revised and retitled "The Orchard Keeper" in *Selected* [137]); "this body . . . made of energy compacted and whirling" ("We Love This Body" [51], slightly revised in *Selected* [138]); and "a new age" which "comes close through the dark" ("Wings Folding Up" [53], revised and retitled "Glimpse of the Waterer" in *Selected* [139]).

The two final poems, "Snowed In" and "The Cry Going Out over Pastures," need to be looked at more closely. Both of these poems document moments of illumination in a world running down.

"Snowed In" (55–56), is one of several poems near the end of *This Body* that picks up Bly's pervasive snow symbolism. It begins:

It is the third day of snow. Power has been out
since yesterday. The horses stay in the barn. At four

THE MORNING GLORY AND *THIS BODY IS MADE OF CAMPHOR AND GOPHERWOOD*

> I leave the house, sinking to my waist in snow, and push open the study door. Snow falls in. I sit down at the desk, there is a plant in blossom.

Here, on "the third day of snow," symbol of a natural resurrection, the poet finds a plant of two petals (cf. the "double flower" in the previous poem, "Wings Folding Up" [53]) in blossom. These two petals become "two tendernesses looking at each other . . . longing to be blown" or "shaken, to circle slowly upward, or sink down toward roots." Thus "the snow and the orangey blossoms are both the same flow . . . at home when one or two are present" and they are also symbolic of the anonymous "man and woman" who "sit quietly near each other" and who quickly become "us," who, joined by their bodies in the only way that man and woman can really join, equal the elements "in energy" and are able to sing:

> A man and woman sit quietly near each other. In the snowstorm millions of years come close behind us, nothing is lost, nothing rejected, our bodies are equal to the snow in energy. The body is ready to sing all night, and be entered by whatever wishes to enter the human body singing. . . . (Bly's ellipsis)

This is the body that the whole of *This Body* celebrates.

The final poem, "The Cry Going Out over Pastures" (59, revised in *Selected* 140) is, not surprisingly, a love poem. It begins, "I love you so much with this curiously alive and lonely body." Love can counter death if it follows its inevitable, inherently religious impulse and if it sees, in the celebrations of the body, a symbolic association with the celebration of the soul. "There is death but also this closeness . . . this joy when the bee rises into the air . . . to find the sun, to become the son. . . ." When the bee rises into the air to find the "sun" in order to become the "son," the poem has moved from the physical to the metaphysical and the mystical. This is very much what many of the poems of *This Body* have attempted to do—to rise up to a body beyond the physical body, to define and finally to name what is, outside of the poetry, unnameable. The book ends with a question and an answer:

> What shall I say of this? I say, praise to the first man who wrote down this joy clearly, for we cannot remain in love with what we cannot name. . . . (Bly's ellipsis)

Here, in *This Body*, Bly names what he loves.

Notes

1. Bly, *Talking* 115.
2. Robert Bly, *The Morning Glory* (New York: Harper & Row, 1975); *This Body is Made of Camphor and Gopherwood* (New York: Harper & Row, 1977). Hereafter, references to these books will be included in the text.

3. Bly, *Selected* 202.

4. "About the Author," *This Body* 61.

5. Bly, *Selected* 130.

6. Bly, *Morning Glory* [xiii].

7. Bly, *News of the Universe* 210.

8. Bly, "The Mind Playing," *Singular Voices: American Poetry Today,* ed. Stephen Berg (New York: Avon Books, 1985) 17.

9. Molesworth, *Fierce Embrace* 132.

10. Anthony Libby, *Mythologies of Nothing: Mystical Death in American Poetry 1940-70* (Urbana: University of Illinois Press, 1984) 180.

11. Russell Edson, "The Prose Poem in America," *Parnassus: Poetry in Review,* 5:1 (Fall/Winter, 1976): 322, 324. See also Edson's "Portrait of the Writer as a Fat Man: Some Subjective Ideas or Notions on the Care & Feeding of Prose Poems," *Field* 13 (Fall, 1975): 19-29.

12. See William V. Davis's " 'In a Low Voice to Someone He is Sure is Listening': Robert Bly's Recent Poems in Prose," *The Midwest Quarterly* 25:2 (Winter, 1984): 149-152.

13. Michael Benedikt, *The Prose Poem: An International Anthology* (New York: Dell 1976) 48-49, 41-42. Jonathan Monroe's recent study of the "genreless genre" of the prose poem quite correctly describes Bly's relationship to this genre, which historically has been a "genre of revolt," as a drawing away from his political poetry, a "depoliticiz [ation of] what has been historically a highly charged, polemical, form-smashing genre for the sake of ecstatic religious content and a focus on domestic concerns and the inner life." (*A Poverty of Objects: The Prose Poem and the Politics of Genre* [Ithaca: Cornell University Press, 1987] 301.)

14. Bly, "What the Prose Poem Carries With It," *The American Poetry Review* 6:3 (May/June, 1977): 44.

15. Bly, "What the Prose Poem Carries With It" 44.

16. Ralph J. Mills, Jr. " 'The Body with the Lamp Lit Inside': Robert Bly's New Poems," *Northeast* 3:2 (Winter, 1976-77): 44.

17. Bly, Duffy and James Wright collaborated on *The Lion's Tail and Eyes* (Madison, MN: Sixties Press, 1962).

18. Edson, "Prose Poem" 323.

19. This paraphrase of Whitman (see "Song of Myself" section 32) is significant because Bly has gone through anxiety of influence

experiences with Whitman, both personally and poetically. Perhaps Bly's most interesting substantial statement on Whitman is his "What Whitman Did Not Give Us." (Perlman, Folsom and Campion, eds. *Walt Whitman: The Measure of His Song* [Minneapolis: Holy Cow! Press, 1981] 321–334.)

20. Stephen Mitchell, ed. and trans., *The Selected Poetry of Rainer Maria Rilke* (New York, Vintage Books, 1984) 193–195; see also 329.

21. Anthony Libby points out that Bly often uses herons, which have been "imagined as angelic for centuries," along with the sea lions and boulders, "to create a sense of visible, realistically described landscape that contains an immediately felt sense of the invisible." ("Dreaming of Animals," *Plainsong* 3 [Fall, 1981]: 53.)

22. Bly, "What the Prose Poem Carries With It" 45.

23. Bly, "The Mind Playing" 17.

24. Bly, "What the Prose Poem Carries With It" 45.

25. Gaston Bachelard, *The Poetics of Reverie: Childhood, Language, and the Cosmos,* trans. Daniel Russell (Boston: Beacon Press, 1971) 173.

26. Molesworth, *Fierce Embrace* 129, 134. Even a critic like Philip Dacey who is quite critical of *This Body* finds it to be "emphatically a book of deep religious longing." (See Dacey, "This Book Is Made of Turkey Soup and Star Music," *Parnassus: Poetry in Review* 7 [Fall/ Winter, 1978]: 34.)

27. Bly has, on several occasions, talked of form in poetry in terms of a snail shell. In "The Prose Poem as an Evolving Form," he says: "What is the prose poem's relation to form? I feel that form in art relies on form in nature for its model, and form in nature amounts to a tension between private spontaneity and the hard impersonal. The snail gives its private substance to its private skin or shell, but the shell's curve is utterly impersonal, and follows the Fibonacci sequence. Form in poetry follows this model." (*Selected,* 202; cf. Bly, "Form that is Neither In nor Out" in Jones and Daniels, *Solitude and Silence* 24.)

28. Molesworth, *Fierce Embrace* 132.

29. D. H. Lawrence, *Psychoanalysis and the Unconscious* (New York: Thomas Seltzer, 1923) 51.

THE MORNING GLORY AND *THIS BODY IS MADE OF CAMPHOR AND GOPHERWOOD*

30. C. G. Jung, *Modern Man in Search of a Soul,* trans. W. S. Dell and Cary F. Baynes (New York: Harcourt, Brace & World, 1966) 11, 15.

31. C. G. Jung, *Two Essays on Analytical Psychology* 115.

32. In his "three brain" essay Bly says, "If there is no central organization to the brain, it is clear that the three brains must be competing for all the available energy at any moment," and "spiritual growth for human beings depends on our ability to transfer energy" (*Leaping Poetry* 62, 64).

33. Here one should remember the "dragons" in several of Bly's poems and the "dragon smoke" in his essay, "Looking for Dragon Smoke," which "means that a leap has taken place in the poem"—which "can be described as a leap from the conscious to the unconscious" part of the mind (*Leaping Poetry* 1)—as well as the "dragon" referred to in "I Came Out of the Mother Naked," which "in inner life is man's fear of women, and in public life . . . is . . . matriarchy's conservative energy." (*Sleepers* 30) Cf. Jung's statement that "in certain myths . . . there are . . . indications that the hero is himself the dragon" (*Analytical Psychology: Its Theory and Practice* [New York: Pantheon Books, 1968] 102–103).

34. "The Sleeper" is very similar to a poem by Kabir, in a version by Bly. In it we read, "Listen friends, this body is his dulcimer. / He draws the strings tight, and out of it comes the music of the inner universe." (Robert Bly, *The Kabir Book: Forty-Four of the Ecstatic Poems of Kabir* [Boston: Beacon Press, 1977] 46.) Several of the poems in *This Body* are similar to Bly's versions of the ecstatic poems of Kabir.

35. For an interesting comment on this poem, including a possible source in Kabir, see Ralph J. Mills, Jr., "Of Energy Compacted and Whirling: Robert Bly's Recent Prose Poems," *New Mexico Humanities Review* 4:2 (1981): 40–41.

36. At the outset of his *Lives of a Cell* Thomas says, "I have been trying to think of the earth as a kind of organism, but it is no go. . . . If not like an organism, what is it like, what is it *most* like? Then, . . . it came to me: it is *most* like a single cell." (Lewis Thomas, *Lives of a Cell* [New York: Bantam, 1975] 4.)

37. Mills, "Of Energy Compacted and Whirling" 44–45.

38. The tercet has been cut in Bly's revision of "The Origin of the Praise of God" in *Selected* 136.

39. Louis L. Martz, *The Poetry of Meditation: A Study in English Religious Literature of the Seventeenth Century* (New Haven: Yale University Press, 1962) 330.

40. Louis L. Martz, *The Paradise Within: Studies in Vaughan, Traherne, and Milton* (New Haven: Yale University Press, 1964) 177. For more on Martz and meditation and the relation of meditation to the mystical in Bly see William V. Davis's "Camphor and Gopherwood": 98–99, 102.

The Man in the Black Coat Turns and *Loving a Woman in Two Worlds*

*T*he *Man in the Black Coat Turns* (1981),[1] Bly's tenth book of poems, took him more than ten years to write. Bly's symbolic turn toward home, the self-referential elegy many writers come to, *Black Coat* describes the end of the journey *Silence in the Snowy Fields* began almost twenty years before. But *Black Coat* is more than a simple return to Bly's personal and poetic origins. Bly constantly circles back to beginnings and, with every return, he discovers another beginning. Just so, *Black Coat* is not an end but another new beginning.

Black Coat shares much of its tone and mood, some of its themes, and many of its sources with *Silence*.[2] It also adds the crucial new development of a more personal voice to Bly's canon. The poems in *Black Coat*, together with its companion volume, *Loving a Woman in Two Worlds* (1985), are Bly's most personal and private poems. As such, they tell a good deal about him now, and about where he has been and where he is going.

133

Black Coat is divided into three sections, the first and third poems in lines, the second, like *Morning Glory* and *This Body,* poems in prose. The prose poems in the central section, which appear almost as carry overs from the earlier books of prose poems, really represent a transitional form. Knowing that he would be dealing with "heavy thought-poems" in *Black Coat,* Bly asks, "What sort of form is proper" for these poems? "Free verse in brief lines doesn't seem right" because it "suggests doubt and hesitation, whereas these thoughts are obsessive, massive, even brutal. And the prose poem form doesn't seem right, because prose poems flow as rivers flow, following gravity around a rock." And since "these thoughts are more like the rocks themselves" they need a new form, "a form that would please the old sober and spontaneous ancestor males." Therefore, Bly "tried to knit the stanzas together in sound, and . . . set [himself] a task of creating stanzas that each have the same number of beats."[3] Although several of the prose poems in this book, "The Dried Sturgeon" (21–22, *Selected* 108), "A Bouquet of Ten Roses" (23–24, *Selected* 107), and "Finding an Old Ant Mansion" (27–30, *Selected* 110–112), in particular, are important poems, only the lined poems in the first and third sections of the book, those "rocks" that create the strongest resistance, and whose "language begins to take on the darkness and engendered quality of matter,"[4] will be considered here.

In one of the prose poems, "Eleven O'Clock at Night," Bly says, "Many times in poems I have

escaped—from myself. . . . Now more and more I long
for what I cannot escape from" (18). That inescapable
essence which the poems in *Black Coat* confront, and
the object poems in prose in the earlier books avoid, is a
depth of personal existence and experience.

In *Black Coat* Bly opens the door of the self to expose
deeper levels of reality. "Snowbanks North of the
House" (3–4, *Selected* 148), the first poem in *Black Coat*,
is an important transitional poem. Like "great sweeps
of snow . . . thoughts that go so far," it goes back to the
beginning, to *Silence.* This poem represents one stage of
the recovery of the shadow which Bly speaks of in *A
Little Book on the Human Shadow*[5] and it also introduces
the dominant theme of *Black Coat*, the father-son relationship.

In "Snowbanks . . ." the initial focus is on the father ("The father grieves for his son and will not leave
the room where the coffin stands" 3), but later the focus
shifts to the son as Bly explores both sides of the father-
son dichotomy. The ending of the poem provides the
title for the book. The references to "the man in the
black coat," the father, and the snow parallel Bly's memory of "My father wearing a large black coat . . . holding a baby up over the snow . . . my brother or myself"
in his essay, "Being a Lutheran Boy-God in Minnesota."
Bly remembers that "always around [his father] there
was a high exhilaration, pursued by grief and depres-
sion," that "he had a gift for deep feeling. Other men
bobbed like corks around his silence." And he comes to
respect his father ("such a beautiful thing!") as a "soli-

tary man" who "is the stone pin that connects this world to the next."[6]

In the second poem, "For My Son Noah, Ten Years Old" (5–6, *Selected* 152), the transition from Bly the speaker as son to Bly the speaker as father has already occurred. Bly says, "The end of the poem suggests that spontaneity reappears in our relationship with our sons when we live in the grief of the return."[7]

The "grief of the return" in terms of the father-son relationship is the theme of the next poem, "The Prodigal Son" (7, *Selected* 147). This theme, as already indicated, runs throughout Bly's work. The poem begins, "The Prodigal Son is kneeling in the husks." Here, even at the outset of the poem, the son is already away from his father, already fallen on hard times, already among the swine ("The swine go on feeding in the sunlight"). The story of the prodigal son is an old story, as is indicated by the references to Tyre and Sidon, cities important in New Testament times, but cities ancient even then, both having been conquered by Alexander the Great, and older even than that (Sidon was one of the most ancient Phoenician cities, founded in the third millenium B.C.). In short, the story is as ancient as the generations of men ("father beyond father beyond father") and as new as the poet's relationship to his own father, who, he says, "is seventy-five years old").

Although this poem is clearly important for Bly's theme, it remains somewhat confusing and enigmatic. The references to the Biblical parable in Luke 15:11–32, to Alexander, the allusion to the Irish folk tale men-

tioned by Yeats in his *Autobiography,* all deal with fathers
and sons and the conflict between them, but the poem
stops short of taking a stand on the relationship or making a specific personal statement. The original final line,
"What we cannot solve is expressed by the swine,"[8] is
indicative of Bly's inability to state his theme clearly; he
"cannot solve" it. The revised last line, "Under the water there's a door the pigs have gone through" (7), links
the end with the beginning of the poem, and has obvious Jungian associations, but does little to define the
dilemma or exorcise the "demons" that possess father-
son relationships.[9]

The theme of the father-son relationship, so important in *Black Coat*, is rather new in Bly's thinking although it is a natural outgrowth of the age we live in as
well as Bly's interest in myth, fairy tales, Jungian psychology, and his own personal background as a "boy
god." Bly has discussed in depth what might be seen as
the background to the poems in *Black Coat* on several
occasions. Here is a summary of his views: "Historically, the male has changed considerably in the past
thirty years." The 1950s male "was vulnerable to collective opinion" and "lacked feminine space . . . lacked
compassion, in a way that led directly to the unbal-
anced pursuit of the Vietnam war. . . . Then, during the
'60s, another sort of male appeared." The war "made
men question what an adult male really is. And the
women's movement encouraged men" until "some men
began to see their own feminine side and pay attention
to it." Still, the "grief and anguish in the younger males

was astounding" and "part of the grief was remoteness from their fathers." Now, "it's possible that men are once more approaching [the] deep male" in the psyche, "the *deep* masculine." "When a boy talks with the hairy man, he is . . . getting into a conversation . . . about something wet, dark, and low—what James Hillman would call 'soul.' And I think that today's males are just about ready to take that step" and be initiated "into the moistness of the swampy fathers who stretch back century after century. . . . After a man has done some work in recovering his wet and muddy feminine side, often he still doesn't feel complete. A few years ago I began to feel diminished by my lack of embodiment of the fruitful male, or the 'moist male.' I found myself missing contact with the male—or should I say my father?. . . . It takes a while for a man to overcome" his mother. "The absorption with the mother may last ten, fifteen, twenty years, and then rather naturally, a man turns toward his father."[10] This statement rather clearly summarizes Bly's poetic activity from his beginnings up to the moment of *Black Coat* and through it.

This focus on the father as the first "transformer" of his son's energies is, ideally, followed by exposure to a "wise old man," who "assumes the role of a shaman" and teaches the boy "artistic curiosity and intellectual discipline, values of spirit and soul, the beginnings of a rich inner life." This stage should be followed by an "intensive study of mythology." As Keith Thompson says, "Bly became interested in these themes when his own sons began to grow up, and when, after years of emo-

THE MAN IN THE BLACK COAT TURNS AND
LOVING A WOMAN IN TWO WORLDS

tional distance, he began to get close to his own father."[11] Bly reports that "the American man is often 40
or 45 before the . . . events of initiation have taken
place completely enough to be felt as events." The final
stage in the process is "a deepening of feeling toward
the religious life."[12]

The first section of *Black Coat*, following the initial
poems on the literal father-son relationship, concludes
with an elegy on Neruda. Bly wrote "Mourning Pablo
Neruda" (11-13, revised in *Selected* 149-151) "in [Neru-
da's] skinny pitch-enlivened form . . . to honor" the
"old reckless dead" man, "and to honor another, William Carlos Williams, I put rocks into the same poem by
means of an abrupt line break" (*Selected* 144). Williams,
and especially Neruda, are crucial "father-figures" for
Bly,[13] and, as he says in the poem, "the dead remain
inside / us" (12).

The third section of *Black Coat* opens with "The
Grief of Men" (33-34), an important poem for the
theme of the entire book. The poem begins with a
"Buddhist" who "ordered his boy to bring him, New
Year's / morning, a message . . . / he himself had written." The "message," delivered on the first morning of
the New Year reads:

> "Busyness has caught you, you have slowed
>   and stopped.
> If you start toward me, I
> will surely come
> to meet you."

UNDERSTANDING ROBERT BLY

The man weeps. Then the poem moves out into nature. The poet hears a "coot" call his Keatsian "darkening call," a "dog's doubt," and sees a silent porcupine, and "fresh waters" that "wash past the tidal sands, / into the delta . . . and are gone." The poem ends with a very personal reference to Bly's Aunt Bertha who died in childbirth and of her husband who "will not lie quiet" but "throws himself against the wall." The uncle is comforted and cared for by men:

> Men come to hold him down.
> My father is there,
> sits by the bed long night after night.

Here, in the figure of the poet's father being there, and caring for another man, Bly makes the first overt reference to the importance and significance of men for other men in this book. The "grief of men" has been traced to a specific personal context, and this poem is a moving introduction to the dominant theme of this section of the book—indeed, to the book as a whole.

"Words Rising" (42–44, revised in *Selected* 169–170), is the prelude to a hymnlike crescendo, the most beautiful musical conclusion in all of Bly's canon, to which the end of *Black Coat* builds. (Bly places "Words Rising" last in the section of poems from *Black Coat* in his *Selected* poems.)

"Words Rising" begins: "I open my journal, write a few / sounds with green ink, and suddenly / fierceness enters me." Then, "the music comes." This fierce music, the way words make and remake the world ("Watery

THE MAN IN THE BLACK COAT TURNS AND
LOVING A WOMAN IN TWO WORLDS

syllables come welling up. . . . / The old earth fragrance remains / in the word 'and.' We experience / 'the' in its lonely suffering. . . . / When a man or woman feeds a few words / with private grief, the shames we knew / before we could invent the wheel, / then words grow. . . . / We see a crowd with dusty / palms turned up inside each / verb" [*Selected* 169–170) is the subject of this poem. In the final stanza the words do almost "rise" to a kind of prayer for the world.

> Blessings then on the man who labors
> in his tiny room, writing stanzas on the lamb;
> blessings on the woman who picks the brown
> seeds of solitude in afternoon light
> out of the black seeds of loneliness.
> And blessings on the dictionary maker, huddled among
> his bearded words, and on the setter of songs
> who sleeps at night inside his violin case.
>
> (*Selected* 170)[14]

"A Meditation on Philosophy" (46–47, revised in *Selected* 162–163) looks backward to literal and poetic ancestors and forward to poetic progeny yet to come. It begins with an evocation of Yeats's "The Wild Swans of Coole" and "A Prayer for My Daughter" as Marjorie Perloff has pointed out[15] and the Chinamen "exchanging poems" in stanza four may refer to Yeats's Chinamen in "Lapis Lazuli."[16]

The "restless gloom in my mind" is prelude to the philosophic "meditation" of the rest of the poem. The last two stanzas look forward to the "father" poems still to come in this book and back both to the feminine in *Sleepers* and elsewhere and forward to *Loving a Woman in Two Worlds.* The "thunderstorms longing to come / into the world through the minds of women" and the dream of the father as "an enormous turtle" suggest the "momentary hope that the side of feminine consciousness . . . call[ed] the Ecstatic Mother will return. . . . The turtle is one of the Mother's favorite creatures; the father's metamorphosis thus spells out the return of matriarchy" even though "the text never quite connects the case of Bly's father . . . to the thesis that the Mother consciousness . . . is destroying masculinity."[17] Still, the fact that the father as turtle is "enormous," that his eyes are "open" and that he is "lying on the basement floor" suggests that the grounding for the power and the basis of the final vision will be with the father.[18] In "Four Ways of Knowledge" (51–54, revised in *Selected* 164–167) Bly talks of the "Wild Man" who "turns men to turtles" (53).

As Bly says regarding meditation, "The West misunderstands 'meditation' or sitting because it assumes that the purpose of meditation is to achieve unity. On the contrary, the major value of sitting . . . is to let the sitter experience the real chaos of the brain."[19]

The "meditation" of "A Meditation on Philosophy" serves as a kind of introduction to the next poem, "My Father's Wedding" (48–50, revised in *Selected* 153–155), a poem important to the theme of the book. The most explicit poem, before *Black Coat*, to suggest the quest that is the theme of this book is entitled, appropriately enough, "Finding the Father" (see Chapter Three). In "Finding the Father" the poet begins the search for the father, who "lonely in his whole body" is "waiting for you" (*This Body* 19).

"My Father's Wedding" begins,

> Today, lonely for my father, I saw
> a log, or branch,
> long, bent, ragged, bark gone.
> I felt lonely for my father when I saw it.

The second through fifth stanzas are an enigmatic and awkward "meditation" on the "invisible limp" which "some men live with." This invisible flaw will become visible no matter how hidden: "If a man, cautious, / hides his limp, / Somebody has to limp it! Things / do it; the surroundings limp." Bly says of himself, "I learned to walk swiftly, easily, / no trace of a limp." And, punning on his "leaping" poetry, "I even leaped a little." But then asks, "Guess where my defect is?" Bly's legacy from his father, from the generations of fathers, the "limp" passed down to him, is what he will shortly characterize as "noble loneliness."

After this rather awkward "meditation," the poet moves to a powerful account of his father's wedding:

> On my father's wedding day,
> no one was there
> to hold him. Noble loneliness
> held him. Since he never asked for pity
> his friends thought he
> was whole. Walking alone he could carry it.

He came in limping. It was a simple
wedding, three
or four people. The man in black,
lifting the book, called for order.
And the invisible bride
stepped forward, before his own bride.

He married the invisible bride, not his own.
In her left
breast she carried the three drops
that wound and kill. He already had
his bark-like skin then,
made rough especially to repel the sympathy

he longed for, didn't need, and wouldn't accept.
So the Bible's
words are read. The man in black
speaks the sentence. When the service
is over, I hold him
in my arms for the first time and the last.

After that he was alone
and I was alone.
Few friends came; he invited few.
His two-story house he turned
into a forest,
where both he and I are the hunters.

(Selected 154–155)

This poem, dated 1924, is immediately interesting
because its speaker will not be born until 1926. Clearly,
the account, which seems to be a literal account of the

wedding, has thrown over it the trappings of myth and
depth psychology. The "invisible bride" who carries the
"three drops / that wound and kill" in her breast, the
bride the father marries instead of his own literal bride,
is a spectral figure drawn in dream and related to myth.
It is fairly clear that Bly has drawn heavily on the fairy
tale "Faithful John" for some of the details in this
poem.[20] Like the poem, "Faithful John" tells the story of
a literal and surrogate father-son relationship, of a mar-
riage in which the bride carries three drops of blood in
her breast, and of Faithful John who is turned to stone
(as opposed to the "bark-like skin" of the father in the
poem—although the log at the beginning of the poem,
"ragged, bark gone," is similar to stone in appearance).

Marie-Louise van Franz says that the "Faithful
John" fairy tale "mirrors masculine psychology." In an
extended commentary on the tale she discusses the "archetypal" theme of this story in which a bride, "con-
taminated with unconscious impulses which want
to become conscious and, because they are not, . . . get
at the man's emotional side and influence his
moods . . . so [that] he has to cross the bridge of his
emotions to find out what the demonic powers are,"
discovers that "generally they are mainly religious
ideas."[21]

Faithful John "is the representative of the transcen-
dent function" and "like Khidr," the "first angel of the
throne of Allah" in the 18th Sura of the Koran, "is a
representative of the divine principle of the unconscious."[22] In both the theological and the psychological

UNDERSTANDING ROBERT BLY

senses of the term, "religious ideas" are predominant at the end of Bly's poem and they are made even more conspicuous in the revision in *Selected*. The "Bible's / words are read" ("So / the words are read" in the *Black Coat* version) and "The man in black / speaks the sentence." On the one hand, this is simply a reference to the "sentence" of a wedding ceremony ("I now pronounce you . . ."); on the other hand, it suggests some sort of punishment, a "sentence" to a life of loneliness, without friendship, which is passed down from generation to generation while the world becomes a kind of forest where men seek for something they never find.

The final three poems in *Black Coat* form a thematic triptych. "Fifty Males Sitting Together" (55–57, revised in *Selected* 145–146)[23] seems to begin where "My Father's Wedding" left off and it anticipates the final poem in the book, "Kneeling Down to Look into a Culvert." In "Fifty Males Sitting Together," "After a long walk in the woods" the poet "turn[s] home, drawn to water." Then the poet finds a "coffinlike shadow," "a massive / masculine shadow," of "fifty males sitting together / . . . lifting something indistinct / up into the resonating night," softening "half" the small lake. The sunlight on "the water still free of shadow, / . . . glows with the high / pink of wounds" (*Selected* 145). Clearly, there is something of rites of initiation here. As Bly says elsewhere, "We can . . . imagine initiation as that moment when the older males together welcome the younger male into the male world."[24]

THE MAN IN THE BLACK COAT TURNS AND LOVING A WOMAN IN TWO WORLDS

Then the scene rather abruptly shifts to "the son who lives / protected by the mother," who:

> loses courage,
> goes outdoors to feed with wild
> things, lives among dens
> and huts, eats distance and silence;
> he grows long wings, enters the spiral, ascends.
>
> How far he is from working men when he is done!
> From all men! The males singing
> chant far out
> on the water grounded in downward shadow.
> He cannot go there because
> he has not grieved
> as humans grieve. If someone's
> head was cut
> off, whose was it?
> The father's? Or the mother's? Or his?
> The dark comes down slowly, the way
> snow falls, or herds pass a cave mouth.
> I look up at the other shore; it is night.

(*Selected* 146)

This "dark night" here at the end of the poem is one of the main threads which run throughout all of Bly's work. In the third of the "Six Winter Privacy Poems" "the darkness appears as flakes of light" (*Sleepers* 3); but the image goes back to Bly's beginnings in *Silence* where he speaks of "a darkness [that] was always there, which we never noticed" (*Silence* 60). And the "thin

man with no coat" riding "the horse of darkness
. . . fast to the east" (*Silence* 52) is the first prefiguration
of the man who dons a black coat and dies fighting at
the end of this book.

"Crazy Carlson's Meadow" (58–60, revised in *Selected* 160–161) is one of the most complex poems Bly
has written. It brings together a cluster of images
which, in the aggregate, define much of what he is
about in *Black Coat* and in his work as a whole. The
poem begins simply enough, with the story of "Crazy
Carlson," who "cleared his meadow alone / . . . back to
the dark firs" which "make sober / . . . deathlike"
caves, "inviting as the dark- / lidded eyes of . . .
women . . . who live in bark huts (*Selected* 160). But in
these caves:

> There is no room
> for the dark-lidded boys who longed to be Hercules.
> There is no room even for Christ.
> He broke off
> his journey toward the Father,
> and leaned back into the Mother's fearful tree.
>
> (*Selected* 160)

Even Christ's first miracle, the turning of the water into
wine at the wedding in Cana (see John 2:1–11), is
"refused" ("the wine of Cana turned back to vinegar")
and Christ's life "broken / on the poplar tree," like a
leaf fallen, has no efficacious effect or abiding significance: "your inner horse . . . galloped away / into the
wind without / you, and disappeared / into the blue

sky. Your horse never reached your father's house" (59)
and thus "all consequences" are "finished."

> Now each young man wanders in the sky alone,
> ignoring the absent
> moon, not knowning
> where ground is, longing once more for the learning
> of the fierce male who hung for nine days only
> on the windy tree.
> Beneath his feet
> there is darkness; inside the folds of darkness words
>   hidden.

The "fierce male" referred to here is Odin, the "All-father," the Norse god who agreed to self-sacrifice on the World Tree, Yggdrasill, in order to acquire the wisdom of the runes. In the *Hávamál* (the Words of the High One) of the *Elder Edda*, a 13th century collection of Norse and Icelandic poems, Odin records his own crucifixion: "I know that I hung / on the windswept tree / for nine full nights / . . . myself to myself / . . . I grasped the 'runes' / . . . Then I began to be fruitful / and to be fertile, / to grow and to prosper; / one word sought / another word from me / one deed sought / another deed from me."[25] Odin's success in achieving the runes, the magical written words that make him an even more powerful god and a poet (Odin is also the god of poetry) able to perform magic with words heretofore hidden in darkness would obviously appeal to a poet who has categorized himself as a boy-god and who wishes, with "fierceness," like this "fierce male" god Odin, to let "words rise."[26]

The final poem of *Black Coat*, "Kneeling Down to Look into a Culvert" (61–62, retitled "Kneeling Down to Peer into a Culvert" in *Selected* 168) is a fitting conclusion to the many themes of the book, what one critic has called "a successful poem in the rather rare genre of the archetypal memory, original because it shows the perspective of the parent who will be replaced."[27] It is the "simple," straightforward poem of a family man, a father, thinking through his life, past, present and future. It begins:

> I kneel down to peer into a culvert.
> The other end seems far away.
> One cone of light floats in the shadowed water.
> This is how our children will look when we are dead.

Here, mentioned again, are a series of things that run throughout the book, throughout the whole of Bly's work: the "kneeling," the "light" floating, the "shadowed water," the "children," the "blue sky" of the next stanza. Indeed, the opening line of the second stanza, "I kneel near floating shadowy water," containing four of his most definitive value words, may be the most succinct, quintessential line in all of Bly.

The poet, having "fathered so many children," wonders, "Are they all born?" One cannot help but read this metaphorically as well as literally, the poet wondering about his poetic "progeny," as he "returns" to the "lake newly made," symbol of the unconscious, and becomes a "water-serpent, throwing water drops / off my head, . . . gray loops trail[ing] behind me" (like "long

tails of dragon smoke"?), until "one morning," like the
Odin all-father figure the poet has become, when "a
feathery head pokes from the water / I fight—it's time—
it's right—and am torn to pieces fighting" (62).

As Boehme said, "all beings move onward until the
end finds the beginning" and "the beginning . . . swal-
lows the end" and thus "beginning and end turn back
into unity."[28]

Thus, here at the end of *Black Coat*, in a ritual that
symbolizes a sacrificial death as prelude to a new birth,
the poet, like the man in the black coat, fulfills all the
implications of the final word of the book's title, and
turns.

* * *

Loving a Woman in Two Worlds[29] is Bly's most recent book
of poetry, the prelude to his *Selected Poems*. *Loving* is
divided into three sections, the first and last containing
twelve poems each, the central section twenty-six. Almost half of the poems are eight lines long or less, and
eleven of them are only four lines each. Most of the
poems are love poems in one way or another. Several of
them are explicit sexual poems and many of the others
are symbolically sexual. For Bly this is a book of joy,
celebrating the love between a man and a woman (three
of the poems begin, "A man and a woman . . .") and a
man and his family and the family of man. Thus, thematically, the poems court sentimentality, and some
succumb to it.

In his introduction to the section of poems from
Loving in *Selected*, Bly tries to define the fine line that

keeps love poems from going "out of tune." "If the poem," he says, "veers too far toward actual events, the eternal feeling is lost in the static of our inadequacies; if we confine the poem only to what we feel, the other person disappears" (*Selected* 172). These are thematic considerations. It is the poetic considerations not mentioned by Bly which often cause the poems in *Loving* to go "out of tune."

Perhaps the most obvious theme poem in the book is "A Third Body" (19, retitled "A Man and a Woman Sit Near Each Other" in *Selected* 181) which appears near the end of the first section.

> A man and a woman sit near each other, and
>   they do not long
> at this moment to be older, or younger, nor born
> in any other nation, or time, or place.
> They are content to be where they are, talking or
>   not-talking.
> Their breaths together feed someone whom we
>   do not know.
> The man sees the way his fingers move;
> he sees her hands close around a book she hands
>   to him.
> They obey a third body that they share in
>   common.
> They have made a promise to love that body.
> Age may come, parting may come, death will
>   come.
> A man and a woman sit near each other;
> as they breathe they feed someone we do not
>   know,

> someone we know of, whom we have never
> seen.

The "third body" that the man and woman "share in
common" and "have made promises to love," the un-
seen presence that unites them and unites them with all
other men and women, is what Bly is trying to describe
in many of the poems in *Loving.* Sometimes it is sex and
sometimes it is spirit; usually it is the two mixed together, but always the spiritual predominates. In many
ways this "third body" is similar to the "body not yet
born" in *Light.* The metaphor runs throughout *Loving*
and concludes in the final poem in the book, "In the
Month of May" (77–78, *Selected* 192), in the lines:

> I love you with what in me is unfinished.
>
> I love you with what in me is still
> changing, . . .
> . . . what has not found its body (77).

Loving begins with "Fifty Males Sitting Together"
(3–5), the revision of a poem brought over from *Black
Coat* (55–57).This poem, then, ties *Black Coat* and *Loving*
together and illustrates Bly's obsession with continuity
and his penchant for revision. Still, if *Loving* begins
with a man being initiated both to his own manhood
and maleness, it immediately puts him to the test of
that initiation in the world of men and, especially, in the
world of women.

In rough sequence, the poems in *Loving* follow the
course of a relationship. In "The Indigo Bunting" (6–7,

Selected 175–176), the second poem in the book, the relationship is still distant, casual ("I do not know what will happen. / I have no claim on you" 6) although there is an emotional reaching out on the poet's part:

> I love you where you go
> through the night, not swerving,
> clear as the indigo
> bunting in her flight,
> passing over two
> thousand miles of ocean.

This meeting, and the relationship that results, will be made explicit in the little poem, "The Whole Moisty Night" where the image of the lit lamp from "The Indigo Bunting" is picked up again and the word "wife" implies the consummation of the relationship: "The body meets its wife far out at sea. / Its lamp remains lit the whole moisty night" (10).[30]

The second section of the book begins with "The Roots" (25), a Ramage, a form Bly invented. A Ramage is a poem of eighty-five syllables, distributed among eight lines, in which several sounds are repeated often enough to create an overall tonal structure. "The Roots," a poem about the knowledge of grief and limits, is almost an epistemology of loss. In many ways "The Roots" is a companion poem to "The Grief of Men" in *Black Coat*. Here "the grief of men" is "the love of woman" and this grief, although it "finds roots" in the earth, is limitless. "There are no limits to grief. The loving man / simmers his porcupine stew. Among the tim- / ber growing on earth grief finds roots" (25).[31] What frightens us, as the next poem, "What Frightens Us" (26), says, is that once "we" descend into "some inner, or innermost cave" there is "no beginning or end"—the "grief" of the human condition stretches out limitlessly in all directions.

The basic thematic focus of *Loving* takes Bly in several directions. It leads him to weak or overtly sentimental poems ("The Conditions" 54, and "Seeing You Carry Plants In" 27); to explicit sexual poems ("Ferns" 38, "The Horse of Desire" 65-66, *Selected* 189-190); to moving love poems ("Come with Me" 29 and "In the Month of May" 77-78, *Selected* 192); to poems with the trappings of myth ("Night Frogs" 32-33, "Conversation" 63 and "The Good Silence" 73-74, *Selected* 185-186); and to poems which end in false epiphanies ("At Midocean" 30, *Selected* 179, and "The Artist at Fifty" 52).

Structurally, the book contains examples of most of the forms Bly has worked in throughout his career. There are, as already noted, numerous short, often pithy, poems as well as poems written in "the long Whitman line" (" 'Out of the Rolling Ocean, the Crowd . . .' " 8-9, *Selected* 178 and "Returning Poem" 42-43); poems in short staccato lines ("Two People at Dawn" 14-15, "Love Poem in Twos and Threes" 41 and "A Man and a Woman and a Blackbird" 55-57); poems with literary or artistic associations ("A Man and a Woman and a Blackbird" and "Listening to the Köln Concert" 67-68, *Selected* 191); and poems in the prototypical tripartite manner of many of Bly's earliest poems ("In Rainy September" 17-18, *Selected* 174 and "Alone a

Few Hours" 46–47); even poems that may not quite be poems ("What We Provide" 50).[32]

In short, Bly seems to be trying for a tour de force here in *Loving,* pulling out all the thematic and structural stops. Even if it is understandable that Bly might well have wanted to try for such a tour de force as prelude to his *Selected Poems,* this mechanical decision may be the main reason this book is not more successful.

Nevertheless, several poems in *Loving* need to be looked at specifically. A particularly candid poem is "Night Frogs" (32–33) where, after stating "How much I am drawn toward my parents! I walk back / and forth, looking toward the old landing," he says:

> What is it in my father I keep not noticing?
> I cannot remember years of my childhood.
> Some parts of me I cannot find now.
>
> I intended that; I threw some parts of me away
> at ten; others at twenty; a lot at twenty-eight.
> I wanted to thin myself out as a wire is thinned.
> Is there enough left of me now to be honest?

Even though the poem begins in a myth-like setting, "I wake and find myself in the woods, far from the castle," Bly seems to be speaking nakedly both about his life and his work in the lines quoted above.

"Alone a Few Hours" (46–47) is a lovely lyric reminiscent of much of Bly's early work but incorporating his more recent interest in myth, fairy stories and Chinese folklore. As Bly describes it, the poem has had a

long history. He says, "This one began about ten years
ago as a prose poem and I liked it as a prose poem and
finally I worked and worked and worked and . . . put it
into stanzas like this in which you count the beats, so
many beats a line and every stanza has to have the same
number. . . . It's a form of craftsmanship; it's more like
making a chest of drawers."[33] Although the stanzas dif-
fer in the number of "beats" (either literal stresses or
syllables) both in the published version and in the version on the tape (which is quite different) Bly's point is
well-taken and his comments reveal several important
concerns of his recent career: his constant, continuing
obsession with revision (which, of course, has been
with him since the beginning) and his increased attention to "craft," a term which, early on, he refused to use
or even to talk about.

"Alone a Few Hours" is filled with Bly's most typical catchwords ("today," "alone," "darkened," "naked,"
"father," "light," "snow," "barn," "rain," "window,"
"shadows," "lake," "writing table," "love," "field
mouse," "stone," "misty") but in this poem he brings
them together gently, melliflously, to create the quintessential Bly lyric.

> Today I was alone a few hours, and slowly
> windows darkened, leaving me alone, naked,
> with no father or uncle,
> born in no country . . . I was a streak of light
> through the sky,
> a trail in the snow behind the field mouse,
> a thing that has

simple desires, and one
or two needs, like a barn darkened by rain.

Something enters from the open window.
I sense it, and turn slightly
to the left. Then I notice
shadows are dear to me, shadows in the weeds
near the lake,
and under the writing table where I sit
writing this.
"The hermit is not here;
he is up on the mountain picking ferns."

That's what the hermit's boy told the visitor
looking for him. Then I realize that I do love,
at last, that the simple
joy of the field mouse has come to me.
I am no longer
a stone pile visited from below
by the old ones.
"It's misty up there . . .
I don't know where he is . . . I don't think you
    can find him."

"In the Month of May" (77–78, *Selected* 192), the final poem in *Loving,* is a fitting conclusion to the book. It
is a love poem in which the speaker begins by seeing
and saying, "how well all things / lean on each other,"
how well the earth, the seasons, the insects, the fish,
the animals all work together. This causes him to "understand / I love you with what in me is unfinished //
. . . with what in me is still / changing . . . / what has

not found its body." This is "the miraculous" which is "caught on this earth," even though it continues to contain trappings of the otherworld, and even though it is "not yet born." Here Bly explicitly refers to his early poem, "Looking into a Face" (*Light* 53), and evokes the notion so important in all of his work—that of rising to a "body not yet born," which exists "like a light around the body" giving off an aura that makes man more than what he seems to be. The reference to Gabriel (the "man of God" in Hebrew), the archangel who helps Daniel to understand his vision and who tells him that "at the time of the end" there "*shall be* the vision" (Daniel 8:15–17), who foretells the birth of John the Baptist (Luke 1:11–20) and announces the conception of Jesus to Mary (Luke 1:26–38), seems to suggest the possibility of an announcement or a vision here at the end of this book. The vision, if it is one, is secular, earthbound, earthy and specific, a reference to the "holy bodies" of "lovers" who are seeking "places / . . . to spend the night."

Thus, *Loving,* and Bly's work to date, fittingly ends with a poem that celebrates that which "is still changing," that which is "unfinished."

Notes

1. Robert Bly, *The Man in the Black Coat Turns* (New York: Dial Press, 1981). Hereafter, references to this book will be included in the text.

2. For parallels between *Black Coat* and *Silence* see William V. Davis's, " 'Still the Place Where Creation Does Some Work on Itself': Robert Bly's Most Recent Work," in Joyce Peseroff, ed. *Robert Bly: When Sleepers Awake* (Ann Arbor: University of Michigan Press, 1984) 238–241.

3. Bly, *Selected* 143–144. These seemingly rigid requirements are often difficult to distinguish in many of the poems.

4. Bly, *Selected* 144. In referring to these poems as "rocks" Bly surely must be thinking of Stevens's late dominant poem, *his* final turn toward home, "The Rock," "the habitation of the whole," "the starting point . . . and the end," "the gate / to the enclosure." (See *The Collected Poems of Wallace Stevens* [New York: Random House, 1954] 528.) And one cannot but remember, in this same context, the little poem, "Late Moon" in *This Tree* (57) whose "rocks . . . hum at early dawn." "Late Moon," with its "light over my father's farm" and the poet's "shadow" which "reach[es] for the latch" of his father's door, seems to anticipate, in several significant ways (as already suggested above) the poems in *Black Coat.*

5. Bly, *Book on the Human Shadow* 31–32.

6. Robert Bly, "Being a Lutheran Boy-God in Minnesota," in *Growing Up in Minnesota: Ten Writers Remember Their Childhoods,* ed. Chester Anderson (Minneapolis: University of Minnesota Press, 1976) 205, 217. This essay is a particularly important essay for much of Bly's recent work.

7. Bly, *Book on the Human Shadow* 33.

8. See *The New Republic* 31 Jan. 1981: 28.

9. In this final line Bly alludes to the story in Matthew 8:28–32 in which Jesus casts devils into a herd of swine who then run headlong into the sea as if the water were a door. Bly associates this Biblical story with the Persephone myth, also alluded to in "A Bouquet of Ten Roses" (24). In one account of this myth Persephone is accompanied into Hades by a herd of pigs. Bly refers to the "astonishing detail" of the pigs in the Persephone story and says, "There is a great power in that, and it is somehow related to the pigs Christ drove over the cliff." (See Bly, "Recognizing the Image as a Form of Intelligence," *Field:* 26.)

THE MAN IN THE BLACK COAT TURNS AND
LOVING A WOMAN IN TWO WORLDS

10. Keith Thompson, "What Men Really Want: Interview with Robert Bly," *New Age* 7 (May, 1982): 31, 33–36, 50–51. One new source for Bly's thinking, mentioned here, is James Hillman, the Jungian analyst whose work, especially in books like *The Myth of Analysis: Three Essays in Archetypal Psychology* (1972), *Re-Visioning Psychology* (1975), and *The Dream and the Underworld* (1979), has had a definitive influence on Bly's recent thinking.

11. Keith Thompson, "Robert Bly on Fathers and Sons," *Esquire* 101 (Apr. 1984): 238.

12. Robert Bly, "Men's initiation rites," *Utne Reader* (Apr./May, 1986): 45, 48–49.

13. Bly visited Williams in 1959. In "Sea Water Pouring Back over Stones" in *Morning Glory,* in a passage using a similar metaphor to the one he uses here, Bly refers to "the gentleness of William Carlos Williams after his strokes" (50). In 1964 Bly met Neruda in Paris and, of course, some of his most important translations are of Neruda.

14. The first words of this stanza are misprinted "Blessing them" in the *Black Coat* text. The "man . . . writing stanzas on the lamb" must be Blake and the "woman, who picks the brown seeds of solitude in afternoon light" is, according to Bly, a reference to Emily Dickinson (see Nelson, *Robert Bly: An Introduction* 229), to whom he has already referred in an earlier poem in this book (see "Visiting Emily Dickinson's Grave with Robert Francis" 25–26), while the "dictionary maker" may well be a reference to J. A. H. Murray, editor of the Oxford English Dictionary, conspicuous for his long beard among the "bearded words" of the Oxford English Dictionary.

15. Marjorie Perloff, "Soft Touch," *Parnassus,* 10:1 (Spring/Summer, 1982): 223.

16. Just as Yeats's "Lapis Lazuli" was "inspired" by a carved stone of the Chinese sculptor sent to Yeats as a present, so Bly's poem seems to have been similarly "inspired" by the painting of *The Six Philosophers* from the "Tang" (T'ang) dynasty. Yeats spoke of his poem as an "heroic cry in the midst of despair," (see *Letters of Poetry from W. B. Yeats to Dorothy Wellesley* [New York: Oxford University Press, 1940] 8) a sentiment Bly might well share about his poem.

17. Perloff, "Soft Touch" 224.

18. The reference to the turtle, the creature "most often and most explicitly connected with luminous revelation," (see Libby, "Dreaming of Animals," *Plainsong*: 51) in Bly's poems, harkens back to "The Turtle" in *Sleepers* (5):

> How shiny the turtle is, coming out
> of the water, climbing the rock, as if
> the body inside shone through!
> As if swift turtle wings swept out of darkness,
> crossed some barriers,
> and found new eyes.

19. Bly, *Leaping Poetry* 63.

20. See *The Complete Grimm's Fairy Tales* (New York: Pantheon Books, 1944) 43–51.

21. Marie-Louise von Franz, *The Feminine in Fairy Tales* (New York: Spring Publications, 1976) 3.

22. Marie-Louise von Franz, *Shadow and Evil in Fairy Tales* (Irving, Texas: Spring Publications, 1980) 69, 72–73. Bly has spoken of the "you" in poetry as: "a primitive initiatory force, female in tone," and as "the inner guide, a Khadir or 'Faithful John,' " as well as "the collective 'God' " (see Robert Bly, *Selected Poems of Rainer Maria Rilke* [New York: Harper & Row, 1981] 8).

23. The *Selected* version of "Fifty Males Sitting Together" differs from the version in *Loving a Woman in Two Worlds*. It introduces the poems in that book.

24. Bly, "What Men Really Want" 36.

25. E. O. G. Turville-Petre, *Myth and Religion of the North: The Religion of Ancient Scandinavia* (London: Weidenfeld and Nicolson, 1964) 42. Campbell associates this "Cosmic Tree" from "immemorial antiquity" (Yggdrasill) with Buddha's Bo Tree (the Tree of Enlightenment) and Christ's "Holy Rood (the Tree of Redemption)" (see Campbell, *Hero With a Thousand Faces* 235, n. 31; 33, n. 37; *passim*).

26. It is worth noting here that Bly published his magazine *The Fifties*, *The Sixties* and *The Seventies* from "Odin House" and that he used as colophon for the magazine an image of Odin in armour, on

horseback, his two ravens, which symbolize thought and memory, accompanying him.

27. Donald Wesling, "The Wisdom Writer," *The Nation* 31 Oct. 1981: 447.

28. See Boehme, *Psychologia Vera, Sämmtliche Werke,* vol. 6, ed. K. W. Schiebler (Leipzig: J. A. Barth, 1846) 18–19.

29. Robert Bly, *Loving a Woman in Two Worlds* (New York: Dial Press, 1985). Hereafter, references to this book will be included in the text.

30. "The Whole Moisty Night" is the title poem of a pamphlet of seven love poems Bly published in 1983. In a tape containing eighteen poems from *Loving,* recorded February 25, 1984, entitled "Loving a Woman in Two Worlds," Bly says about "The Whole Moisty Night," "This is one of the first [four line] ones that I did. It came out completely whole. And it gave me hope and I went and did the rest of them."

31. "Porcupine stew" picks up the reference to a porcupine in "The Grief of Men." Among Bly's many animals, the porcupine is an obvious masculine symbol. But Bly may also be thinking here of Galway Kinnell's poem "The Porcupine" where we read, "In character / he resembles us in seven ways" (see Galway Kinnell, *Body Rags* [Boston: Houghton Mifflin, 1967] 56).

32. On the "Loving" tape Bly says about "What We Provide," "Is it quite a poem? I'm not sure."

33. Bly, "Loving" tape.

BIBLIOGRAPHY

Works by Robert Bly
Books of Poetry—Selected

The Lion's Tail and Eyes: Poems Written Out of Laziness and Silence. Madison, MN: Sixties Press, 1962. With James Wright and William Duffy.

Silence in the Snowy Fields. Middletown, CT: Wesleyan University Press, 1962. London: Jonathan Cape, 1967.

The Light Around the Body. New York: Harper & Row, 1967. London: Rapp & Whiting, 1968.

The Teeth Mother Naked at Last. San Francisco: City Lights Books, 1970.

Jumping Out of Bed. Barre, MA: Barre Publishers, 1973.

Sleepers Joining Hands. New York: Harper & Row, 1973.

Point Reyes Poems. Half Moon Bay, CA: Mudra, 1974.

Old Man Rubbing His Eyes. Greensboro, NC: Unicorn Press, 1974.

The Morning Glory. New York: Harper & Row, 1975.

This Body Is Made of Camphor and Gopherwood. New York: Harper & Row, 1977.

This Tree Will Be Here for a Thousand Years. New York: Harper & Row, 1979.

The Man in the Black Coat Turns. New York: Dial Press, 1981.

Loving a Woman in Two Worlds. New York: Dial Press, 1985.

Selected Poems. New York: Harper & Row, 1986.

Books of Translations—Selected

Twenty Poems of Georg Trakl. Madison, MN: Sixties Press, 1961. With James Wright.

Twenty Poems of César Vallejo. Madison, MN: Sixties Press, 1962. With John Knoepfle and James Wright.

Forty Poems. Juan Ramón Jiménez. Madison, MN: Sixties Press, 1967.

BIBLIOGRAPHY

Twenty Poems of Pablo Neruda. Madison, MN: Sixties Press, 1967. With James Wright. London: Rapp & Whiting, 1968.

I Do Best Alone at Night: Poems by Gunnar Ekelöf. Washington, DC: The Charioteer Press, 1968. With Christina Paulston.

Twenty Poems of Tomas Tranströmer. Madison, MN: Sixties Press, 1970.

Neruda and Vallejo: Selected Poems. Boston: Beacon Press, 1971. With John Knoepfle and James Wright.

Lorca and Jiménez: Selected Poems. Boston: Beacon Press, 1973.

Friends, You Drank Some Darkness. Boston: Beacon Press, 1975.

Twenty Poems: Rolf Jacobsen. Madison, MN: Seventies Press, 1977.

The Kabir Book: Forty-Four of the Ecstatic Poems of Kabir. Boston: Beacon Press, 1977.

Truth Barriers: Poems by Tomas Tranströmer. San Francisco: Sierra Club Books, 1980.

Selected Poems of Rainer Maria Rilke. New York: Harper & Row, 1981.

Times Alone: Selected Poems of Antonio Machado. Middletown, CT: Wesleyan University Press, 1983.

Books Edited by Bly

A Poetry Reading Against the Vietnam War. Madison, MN: Sixties Press, 1966. With David Ray.

Forty Poems Touching on Recent American History. Boston: Beacon Press, 1970.

The Sea and the Honeycomb: A Book of Tiny Poems. Boston: Beacon Press, 1971.

David Ignatow: Selected Poems. Middletown, CT: Wesleyan University Press, 1975.

Leaping Poetry: An Idea with Poems and Translations. Boston: Beacon Press, 1975.

News of the Universe. San Francisco: Sierra Club Books, 1980.

BIBLIOGRAPHY

The Winged Life: The Poetic Voice of Henry David Thoreau. San Francisco: Sierra Club Books, 1986.

Essays and Nonfiction—Selected

"Five Decades of Modern American Poetry." *The Fifties* 1 (1958): 36–39.

"A Wrong Turning in American Poetry." *Choice: A Magazine of Poetry and Photography* 3 (1963): 33–47.

"The Dead World and the Live World." *The Sixties* 8 (1966): 2–7.

"Leaping Up into Political Poetry." *London Magazine* 7 (1967): 82–87.

"Acceptance of the National Book Award for Poetry, March 6, 1968." *Tennessee Poetry Journal* 2 (1969): 14–15.

"American Poetry: On the Way to the Hermetic." *Books Abroad* 46 (1972): 17–24.

"Looking for Dragon Smoke." *The Seventies* 1 (1972): 3–8.

"Poetry of Steady Light." *The Seventies* 1 (1972): 48–49.

"The Three Brains." *The Seventies* 1 (1972): 61–69.

"Wild Association." *The Seventies* 1 (1972): 30–32.

"Developing the Underneath." *American Poetry Review* 2 (1973): 44–45.

"The War Between Memory and Imagination." *American Poetry Review* 2 (1973): 49–50.

"Being a Lutheran Boy-God in Minnesota." In *Growing Up In Minnesota: Ten Writers Remember Their Childhood,* ed. Chester G. Anderson. Minneapolis: University of Minnesota Press, 1976, 205–219.

Talking All Morning. Ann Arbor: University of Michigan Press, 1980.

"Two Stages of an Artist's Life." *Georgia Review* 34 (1980): 105–109.

"Recognizing the Image as a Form of Intelligence." *Field* 24 (1981): 17–27.

167

BIBLIOGRAPHY

The Eight Stages of Translation. Boston: Rowan Tree Press, 1983.
"In Search of an American Muse." *New York Times Book Review*
    22 January 1984.

Works About Bly
Bibliography
Roberson, William H. *Robert Bly: A Primary and Secondary Bibliography.* Metuchen, NJ: Scarecrow Press, 1986. Primary and secondary. Supersedes all previous bibliographies. Indispensable for materials up to 1984.
Books
Friberg, Ingegard. *Moving Inward: A Study of Robert Bly's Poetry.* Göteborg, Sweden: Acta Universitatis Gothoburgensis, 1977. The first book-length study of Bly. Obviously limited to the early career. In a rather mechanical way stresses patterns and images (snow, field, barn) and concepts (place, time, life energy) as representative and conspicuous elements in Bly's poetry.
Jones, Richard and Kate Daniels, ed. *Of Solitude and Silence: Writings on Robert Bly.* Boston: Beacon Press, 1981. Miscellany of new work by Bly as well as essays, memoirs and notes about him and his work. Originally published as a double issue of *Poetry East.*
Nelson, Howard. *Robert Bly: An Introduction to the Poetry.* New York: Columbia University Press, 1984. Detailed introductory and chronological study of Bly's major books of poetry through *Black Coat.* Bly's theories often illuminate the poems in this sympathetic and useful study.
Peseroff, Joyce, ed. *Robert Bly: When Sleepers Awake.* Ann Arbor: University of Michigan Press, 1984. Substantial collec-

tion of important essays (several previously unpublished) and reviews, etc. on Bly and his work.

Sugg, Richard P. *Robert Bly.* Boston: Twayne, 1986. Introductory critical analysis, informed by a "pervasive commitment" to a Jungian interpretation, together with a "close reading" of selected poems from Bly's work through *Black Coat.*

Parts of Books and Selected Articles

Altieri, Charles. "Varieties of Immanentist Experience: Robert Bly, Charles Olsen, and Frank O'Hara." *Enlarging the Temple: New Directions in American Poetry During the 1960's.* Cranbury, NJ: Associated University Presses, 1979. 78–93. Bly's theories and poetry are seen as one of several "self-consciously postmodern" positions of "radical presence" in contemporary American poetry.

Baker, Deborah. "Making a Farm: A Literary Biography of Robert Bly." *Poetry East* 4/5 (1981): 145–189. An interesting and useful biographical essay which suggests parallels between Bly's poetry and poetic theories and his life. Reprinted in Jones and Daniels.

Davis, William V. " 'At the Edges of the Light': A Reading of Robert Bly's *Sleepers Joining Hands.*" *Poetry East* 4/5 (1981): 265–282. *Sleepers,* a poetic, religious and psychological struggle for Bly, synthesizes the themes and styles of *Silence* and *Light.* Reprinted in Jones and Daniels.

_____. " 'Hair in a Baboon's Ear': The Politics of Robert Bly's Early Poetry." *The Carleton Miscellany* 18 (1979–80): 74–84. The "inwardness" of *Silence* is intricately related to the "outward" poems of *Light* through Bly's understanding and use of Boehme.

_____. " 'Still the Place Where Creation Does Some Work on Itself': Robert Bly's Most Recent Work." *Robert Bly: When*

BIBLIOGRAPHY

Sleepers Awake, ed. Joyce Peseroff. Ann Arbor: University of Michigan Press, 1984. 237-246. *Black Coat,* Bly's self-referential elegy, brings him back to his beginnings and thus completes and unifies the journey begun in *Silence.*

Gioia, Dana. "The Successful Career of Robert Bly." *The Hudson Review* 40 (1987): 207-223. An overview of Bly's career which stresses his significance for literary history over his own accomplishments as a poet and translator.

Howard, Richard. " 'Like Those Before, We Move to the Death We Love.' " *Alone With America: Essays on the Art of Poetry in the United States Since 1950.* New York: Atheneum, 1969. 38-48. A rhetorically difficult essay in which Boehme's influence on *Silence* and *Light* is described and discussed. Reprinted in Peseroff.

Kramer, Lawrence. "A Sensible Emptiness: Robert Bly and the Poetics of Immanence." *Contemporary Literature* 24 (1983): 449-462. Bly is most accurately seen not as a poet of "deep images" but as a contemporary example of the tradition of "immanence" which has its source in Whitman.

Libby, Anthony. "Fire and Light, Four Poets to the End and Beyond." *Iowa Review* 4 (1973): 111-126. Bly, Merwin, Dickey and Ted Hughes write poems that explore the spiritual and psychological crises of the collapse of modern culture.

_____. "Robert Bly Alive in Darkness." *Iowa Review* 3 (1972): 78-89. A detailed treatment of the psychological trappings of Bly's theories, especially his Great Mother theory. Reprinted in Peseroff.

_____. "Robert Bly Unknowing Knowing." *Mythologies of Nothing: Mystical Death in American Poetry 1940-1970.* Urbana: University of Illinois Press, 1984. 153-184. Bly's visionary obsessions and his mysticism "enriched and diluted by political and psychological theories" are examined in the context of earlier twentieth-century poets, especially Stevens and Roethke.

Matthews, William. "Thinking About Robert Bly." *Tennessee Poetry Journal* 2 (1969): 49–57. An interesting hodgepodge of ideas on Bly and his work, both poetic and critical. Reprinted in Peseroff.

Mersman, James P. "Robert Bly: Watering the Rocks." *Out of the Vietnam Vortex*. Lawrence: University of Kansas Press, 1974. 113–157. A readable, detailed treatment of Bly's political poetry. Reprinted in Peseroff.

Mills, Ralph J., Jr. " 'Of Energy Compacted and Whirling': Robert Bly's Recent Prose Poems." *New Mexico Humanities Review* 4 (1981): 29–49. Describes the development of the genre of the prose poem and details Bly's contributions, both poetic and theoretical, to it. Reprinted in Peseroff.

———. " 'The Body with the Lamp Lit Inside': Robert Bly's New Poems." *Northeast* 3:2 (1976–1977): 37–47. *Morning Glory* is seen as a "substantial accomplishment" in terms of the genre of the prose poem in contemporary American poetry and in Bly's canon.

Molesworth, Charles. " 'Rejoice in the Gathering Dark': The Poetry of Robert Bly." *The Fierce Embrace: A Study of Contemporary American Poetry*. Columbia: University of Missouri Press, 1979. 112–138. An important essay that focuses on *This Body* in particular but attempts to see Bly's poetry and critical thinking in reciprocal relation throughout his career.

Nelson, Howard. "Welcoming Shadows: Robert Bly's Recent Poetry." *The Hollins Critic* 12 (1975): 1–15. An overview of Bly's work with stress on the prose poems as examples of his finest work.

Richman, Robert. "The Poetry of Robert Bly." *The New Criterion* 5 (1986): 37–46. A critical overview of Bly's complete canon that finds him suffering from "the two worst poetic excesses of the Sixties: politics and solipsism" and finds some of his critics "misconstruing" his work.

Seal, David. "Waking to 'Sleepers Joining Hands'." *Poetry East* 4/5 (1981): 234–263. A useful, detailed analysis of the poem "Sleepers Joining Hands." Reprinted in Jones and Daniels.

INDEX

This index does not include references to material in the notes.

INDEX

INDEX

INDEX

INDEX

INDEX

INDEX